THE
GRAPHIC DESIGNER'S
SOURCEBOOK

THE Graphic Designer's Source BOOK

POPPY EVANS

NORTH LIGHT BOOKS
CINCINNATI, OHIO

00 99 98 97 96   5 4 3 2 1

Library of Congress Cataloging-in-Publication Data

Evans, Poppy
    The graphic designer's sourcebook / by Poppy Evans
        p.   cm.
    Includes index.
    ISBN 0-89134-642-2 (alk. paper)
    1. Graphic arts—United States—Directories. 2 Graphic arts equipment industry—United States—Directories.
    I. Title.
NC999.E82   1996
741.6′025′73—dc20   95-44200
                                                                                                         CIP

Edited by Terri Boemker
Cover and interior designed by Brian Roeth
Cover illustration and chapter opener illustrations by Julie A. Baker

The following page constitutes an extension of this copyright page.

North Light Books are available for sales promotions, premiums and fund-raising use. Special editions or book excerpts can also be created to specification. For details contact: Special Sales Manager, F&W Publications, 1507 Dana Avenue, Cincinnati, Ohio 45207.

ABOUT THE AUTHOR

After graduating from the University of Cincinnati with a degree in Fine Arts, Poppy Evans got her first taste of publishing by functioning as a one-person production staff—writing, editing and laying out a company newsletter. She has worked as a graphic designer and as a magazine art director for *Screen Printing* and *American Music Teacher,* a national association magazine that won many awards under her direction for its redesign and its artfully conceived covers.

She returned to writing and editing in 1989, as managing editor of *HOW* magazine. Since leaving *HOW,* she has written many articles that have appeared in graphic arts-related magazines, including *Print, HOW, Step-By-Step, Publish, Single Image* and *Confetti.* She is the author of several books on graphic design and teaches graphic design and computer publishing at the Art Academy of Cincinnati.

DEDICATION

This book is dedicated to my son, Evan, who continually inspires me to be the best person I can possibly be.

ACKNOWLEDGMENTS

I would especially like to thank Greg Albert and Lynn Haller at North Light Books for helping me during the developmental stages of this book, and Terri Boemker for her input and one more round of editing.

Others who helped me in locating and qualifying products and services are: Dutch Draley, SGIA; Steve Duccilli, Screen Printing; Lynn Jeffery, SEGD; Kurt McQuiston, Art Academy of Cincinnati; Duane Neher, Johnston Paper; and Debra Sexton, Impressions.

Finally, I would like to thank everyone who contributed a visual. All of these individuals went to some trouble to prepare and forward art or photography for this book, particularly Rich Roat of House Industries and Rick Valicenti of Thirst who both deserve special thanks for their contributions.

To everyone who helped with their advice and ideas, my heartfelt thanks.

TABLE OF CONTENTS

INTRODUCTION

Have you ever tried to locate a product or service and found yourself thumbing through countless directories and trade magazines, only to ultimately fall short of finding what you need? Exasperated, you pick up the phone and start calling colleagues looking for answers, and after several hours of playing phone tag, you still haven't been able to locate what you want.

Sound familiar? There's nothing more frustrating than not knowing where to find something you need to complete the job at hand, especially when you're trying hard to meet a deadline and time is precious. That's why *The Graphic Designer's Sourcebook* was created. The categorized listings of products and services in this book were created specifically to satisfy designers who need to tap into a dependable list of resources as quickly as possible.

Within this book you'll find contact information for every major national competition for graphic design and related disciplines; regional listings of stock illustration and photo agencies and what they specialize in; sources for unusual papers, envelopes, pocket folders and other paper products you may not have even known existed; as well as a countless variety of items and services that designers of packaging, signage and other printed materials will want to have access to. There's even a chapter devoted to the constantly evolving field of interactive multimedia design.

Compiling this directory was no easy task. In the course of locating and qualifying products and services, I encountered many endlessly ringing phones, busy signals, snippy operators, and hundreds of voice mail messages. Companies with unattended phone lines and those with rude sales help didn't make the cut for this book. Those firms that did make their way in are well-established businesses with helpful and knowledgeable sales help, or up-and-coming operations that are doing their best to win your business. You can be assured that when you dial any of the numbers in this book, your call will be greeted by a company with a desire to do business with graphic designers.

As the *Whole Earth Catalog* of the industry, *The Graphic Designer's Sourcebook* will function as your single source for all areas of graphic design, replacing many other directories that focus on just one area of design. In fact, it will probably be the directory that you'll reach for next, whenever your Rolodex file doesn't provide a solution to your quest for a product or service. I know that it's already helped me. As I accumulated information for this book, I found myself pulling up completed chapters on my computer on more than one occasion to locate something that I needed.

If you have suggestions for additional listings for this book, or are aware of a product or service that you would like to share with other graphic designers, please let my publisher know so they can be included in the next edition of *The Graphic Designer's Sourcebook*. Forward your ideas (there's a handy form in the back of this book) to:

Editor of *The Graphic Designer's Sourcebook*
North Light Books
1507 Dana Ave.
Cincinnati, OH 45207
Fax: (513) 531-4744

STUDIO EQUIPMENT AND SUPPLIES

OFFICE, ART AND

DRAFTING SUPPLIES

AND COMPUTER

SUPPLIES AND

EQUIPMENT

office furniture

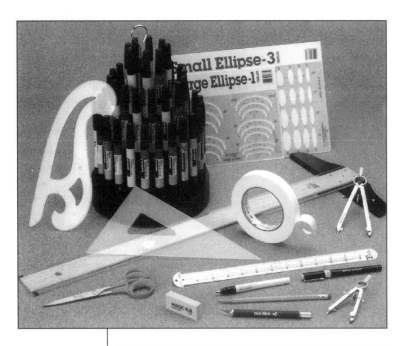

Dick Blick offers a variety of supplies and equipment for graphic artists. The company also sells screen printing and sign-making supplies. For more information, see their listing at right.

ART AND GRAPHIC ART SUPPLIES AND EQUIPMENT

ARTOGRAPH, INC.
13205 16th Ave. N.
Minneapolis, MN 55441
(800) 328-4653, (612) 553-1112
Fax: (612) 553-1262

Manufactures spray booths and opaque projectors.

BADGER AIR-BRUSH CO.
9128 W. Belmont Ave.
Franklin Park, IL 60131
(800) 247-2787 (708) 678-3104
Fax: (708) 671-4352

Manufactures airbrushes and related equipment and supplies. Offers free catalog.

DAIGE
1 Albertson Ave.
Albertson, NY 11507
(800) 645-3323, (516) 621-2100

Offers tabletop waxers and a wax-free adhesive system.

DANIEL SMITH
4150 1st Ave. S.
Seattle, WA 98134
(800) 426-6740, (206) 223-9599
Fax: (206) 223-0672

Catalog available. Offers papers, paints, canvas, brushes, airbrushes, metallic leafing, portfolios and some furniture and studio accessories.

DICK BLICK
Rte. 150, E.
P.O. Box 1267
Galesburg, IL 61401
(309) 343-6181
Fax: (309) 343-5785

Offers an extensive line of art and drafting supplies, furniture, books and software. Also offers screen printing and sign-making supplies. Ask for free catalog.

FIDELITY GRAPHIC PRODUCTS CATALOG
5601 International Pkwy.
P.O. Box 155
Minneapolis, MN 55440-0155
(800) 326-7555, (612) 536-6500
Fax: (800) 842-2725

Technical pens, Pantone specifiers, flat files, drawing tables, punch and bind machines and more. Offers many products below list price. Ask for free catalog.

GRAPHIC ARTS PRODUCTS CORP.
1480 S. Wolf Rd.
Wheeling, IL 60090-6514
(708) 537-9300

Sells dry transfer lettering, borders and other graphic elements. Also offers a line of clip art books. Products are available through art and graphics supply stores.

GTR INDUSTRIES, INC.
7905 Silverton Ave., #113
San Diego, CA 92126
(619) 566-0935

Manufactures spray booths and related equipment.

JOE KUBERT ART & GRAPHIC SUPPLY
37A Myrtle Ave.
Dover, NJ 07801
(201) 328-3266
Fax: (201) 328-7283

Stocks a variety of papers, boards, markers, adhesives and more. Also carries silkscreen supplies, airbrushing equipment, lamps, vinyl letters, and craft supplies such as clay and casting plaster.

LECRO-STIK
3721 Broadway
Chicago, IL 60613
(312) 528-8860
Fax: (312) 528-2874

Sells hand waxers and wax.

LETRASET USA
40 Eisenhower Dr.
Paramus, NJ 07653
(800) 526-9073
Fax: (201) 845-5047

Manufactures markers, pens and studio organizers, comping and imaging systems, and Pantone color papers and films. Also offers software, type, paper, photographic and illustration-specific products, which are described elsewhere in this book. Products are available through art supply stores.

MORSE GRAPHIC ARTS
1938 Euclid Ave.
Cleveland, OH 44115
(216) 621-4175
Fax: (216) 621-0655

Offers tabletop waxers and related supplies.

PAASCHE AIRBRUSH CO.
7440 W. Lawrence Ave.
Harwood Heights, IL 60656
(708) 867-9191
Fax: (708) 867-9198

Airbrushes and related supplies and equipment.

PORTAGE ARTWAXERS
P.O. Box 5500
Akron, OH 44334-0500
(800) 321-2183, (216) 929-4454
Fax: (216) 922-0506

Makes tabletop waxers.

SAX ARTS & CRAFTS
P.O. Box 51710
New Berlin, WI 53151
(800) 323-0388, (414) 784-6880
Fax: (800) 328-4729

Offers paints, brushes, Prismacolor™ pencils, art papers, canvas and more.

UTRECHT MANUFACTURING CORP.
33 35th St.
Brooklyn, NY 11232
(800) 223-9132 (main office and warehouse)
(800) 352-9016 (New York City)
(800) 257-1104 (Philadelphia)
(800) 257-1108 (Boston)
(800) 257-1102 (Washington, DC)
(800) 352-6883 (Detroit)
(800) 352-4638 (Chicago)
(800) 538-7111 (Berkeley, CA)
(800) 961-9612 (San Francisco)

Stocks artist's supplies such as paints, brushes, canvas, etc. Also offers drawing and drafting tools, knives and airbrush equipment. Supplies can be ordered from warehouse as well as store locations in the cities listed above.

CRAFT SUPPLIES AND EQUIPMENT

AMERICAN ART CLAY CO.
4717 W. 16th St.
Indianapolis, IN 46222
(317) 244-6871
Fax: (317) 248-9300

Craft supplies include modeling materials, glitter, fabric dyes and a variety of paints and finishes.

ANYTHING IN STAINED GLASS
1060 Rte. 47 S.
P.O. Box 444
Rio Grande, NJ 08242
(609) 886-0416
Fax: (609) 886-4947

Carries over 14 types of stained glass and stained glass supplies including lamp forms and parts, stencils and pattern books.

BERMAN LEATHERCRAFT
25 Melcher St.
Boston, MA 02210
(617) 426-0870
Fax: (617) 357-8564

Offers all kinds of hides, including deerskin, bat and elk leather. Also carries leather carving tools.

BRIAN'S CRAFTS UNLIMITED
1421 S. Dixie Frwy.
New Smyrna Beach, FL 32168
(904) 672-2726

Stocks T-shirts, visors and other garments, as well as rhinestones, beads, jewelry findings, dried flowers, wreaths, macrame supplies, feathers and more.

NATIONAL ARTCRAFT CO.
23456 Mercantile Rd.
Beachwood, OH 44122
(800) 793-0152, (216) 292-4944
Fax: (800) 292-4916

Extensive collection of electrical items such as lamp parts, kits, chains and prisms. Also stocks clock parts, water globes, kaleidoscope kits, mirrors and jewelry findings.

OFFICE SUPPLIES AND EQUIPMENT

BARDES PRODUCTS, INC.
5245 W. Clinton Ave.
Milwaukee, WI 53223
(800) 959-0402, (414) 354-9000
Fax: (414) 354-1921

Stock and custom vinyl products for protecting and display. Includes slide and transparency holders, job envelopes and more.

BRIDGE INFORMATION SYSTEMS, INC.
121 S. Wilke Rd.
Arlington Heights, IL 60005
(800) 323-0497, (708) 394-3450
Fax: (708) 394-3455

Stocks jumbo-sized envelopes, up to 24″×36″.

FIDELITY DIRECT
5601 International Pkwy.
P.O. Box 155
Minneapolis, MN 55440-0155
(800) 328-3034
Fax: (800) 842-2725

Shipping boxes, mailing tubes and other mailing supplies, including postal scales.

KLEER-VU CUSTOM PRODUCTS
Kleer-Vu Dr.
Brownsville, TN 38012
(800) 365-5827, (901) 772-2500
Fax: (901) 772-4632

Clear vinyl envelopes, ticket holders, etc., for artwork and job holders. Also makes photo and transparency sleeves.

PACKAGING UN-LIMITED, INC.
1121 W. Kentucky St.
Louisville, KY 40210
(502) 584-4331
Fax: (502) 585-4955

Mailing tubes and mailing supplies; packaging materials such as bubble wrap, foam peanuts, etc.

PLASTIC MANUFACTURERS, INC.
3510 Scotts Ln.
Philadelphia, PA 19129-0677
(215) 438-1082
Fax: (215) 438-5560

Clear and colored vinyl envelopes, sleeves and more. (For transparencies, document and job holders, etc.) Customize with printing, embossing, grommets, hangholes, pressure-sensitive backing, etc.

PLASTIC PRODUCTS CO.
P.O. Box 98
Laurel, MD 20725
(800) 882-1022, (301) 953-2222
Fax: (301) 953-9462

Clear vinyl envelopes and sleeves for documents, photos and badges. Also makes zippered portfolios. Offers stock and custom designs hot stamped and silkscreened to your specifications.

SPECTRA COLLECTION
12 South St.
Townsend, MA 01469
(800) 225-9528
Fax: (800) 876-6337

Business forms—invoices, purchase orders, etc.—printable from PC-compatible computers. Forms include carbon and carbonless duplicate copies. Also makes pricing labels, certificates, envelopes, tags, presentation folders and more.

THE TRACIES CO., INC.
100 Cabot St.
Holyoke, MA 01040
(800) 441-7141, (413) 533-7141
Fax: (413) 536-0223

Clear vinyl envelopes for a variety of needs including passbooks, shop envelopes and more. Customize with hot stamping and screen printing.

YAZOO MILLS, INC.
305 Commerce St.
New Oxford, PA 17350
(717) 624-8993
Fax: (717) 624-4420

Mailing tubes in a variety of lengths. Sold by the carton.

PORTFOLIOS

Most art and photography stores stock a standard portfolio: The black "leather" number (or facsimile thereof). This may come with sleeves (or without) bound into a zippered, handled carrier. An alternative is a clamshell box for matted prints and transparencies. The following companies offer the standard portfolios, with a number of variations, as well as portfolios manufactured to your specifications.

BREWER-CANTELMO
116 E. 27th St.
New York, NY 10016
(212) 685-1200
Fax: (212) 689-6457

Offers presentation boxes with a matching portfolio book, clamshell boxes in cloth and leather, presentation mailers and more. Available in a variety of colors, finishes and lining papers. Can create custom designs or customize existing products. Will blind emboss your name on its products.

CENTURY ARCHIVAL PRODUCTS
2419 E. Franklin St.
Richmond, VA 23223
(804) 644-7824

Makes portfolio boxes to fit transparency presentation boards. Not a retail outlet. Call for retailer in your area.

EXECUTIVE EXPRESS
4431 William Penn Hwy.
Murrysville, PA 15668
(800) 837-5554, (412) 733-8695
Fax: (412) 327-6222

Offers zippered portfolios in a wide range of styles and sizes.

SAM FLAX
12 W. 20th St.
New York, NY 10011
(212) 620-3010
Fax: (212) 633-1082

Presentation boxes including clamshell archival boxes with single and dual compartments. A wide range of presentation binders and portfolio cases in a variety of materials.

TEXAS ART SUPPLY
2001 Montrose Blvd.
Houston, TX 77006
(713) 526-5221

Stock portfolios include zippered portfolios, showcase albums and combination presentation cases in a variety of sizes and colors. Several retail outlets in the Houston area. Also takes mail orders.

STUDIO FURNISHINGS

AGIO DESIGNS
19545 NW Von Neumann Dr., Ste. 110
Beaverton, OR 97006
(503) 690-1400
Fax: (503) 690-1423

Manufactures furniture for desktop systems.

ANTHRO
10450 SW Manhasset Dr.
Tualatin, OR 97062
(800) 325-3841, (503) 691-2556
Fax: (800) 325-0045

Manufactures furniture for desktop systems.

FIDELITY GRAPHIC PRODUCTS
5601 International Pkwy.
P.O. Box 155
Minneapolis, MN 55440-0155
(800) 326-7555, (612) 536-6500
Fax: (800) 842-2725

Mail-order house offering flat files, drafting tables, punch and bind machines and more. Offers many products below list price. Ask for free catalog.

Brewer-Cantelmo offers stock presentation boxes with matching portfolio book, clamshell boxes in cloth and leather, presentation mailers and more. The company can also create custom designs or customize existing products. For more information, see their listing under Portfolios at left.

ITC Design Palette is an electronic distribution system that provides the user with instant access to a huge number of electronic graphics products. Does away with browsing catalogs, then phoning, faxing or mailing orders by providing access to products from your desktop, twenty-four hours a day, seven days a week. Products include stock photos, clip art, fonts, video clips, plug-ins and utilities and more. Contact: International Typeface Corp., 866 2nd Ave., New York, NY 10017; (212) 371-0699.

NUARC COMPANY, INC.
6200 W. Howard St.
Niles, IL 60648-3404
(708) 967-4400
Fax: (708) 967-9664

Makes precision-squared tables with built-in light boxes.

ROCONEX
20 Mary Bill Dr.
Troy, OH 45373
(800) 426-6453, (513) 339-2616
Fax: (513) 339-1470

Manufactures vertical filing systems.

SCANCO
P.O. Box 3217
Redmond, WA 98073-3217
(800) 722-6263, (206) 481-5434
Fax: (206) 485-1255

Makes furniture for desktop systems.

WINSTED CORP.
10901 Hampshire Ave. S.
Bloomington, MN 55438-2385
(800) 447-2257, (612) 944-8556
Fax: (612) 944-1546

Furniture for desktop systems.

COMPUTERS AND COMPUTER EQUIPMENT

Contact these computer hardware manufacturers for product information or a local representative in your area. (Note: Fax numbers vary for many of these manufacturers, depending on which division or department the fax is destined for. If you wish to send a fax to a company that does not have a listed fax number, ask the operator for the number of the department you will be faxing to.)

COMPUTER MANUFACTURERS

ALR
9401 Jeronimo St.
Irvine, CA 92718
(800) 444-4ALR, (714) 581-6770
Fax: (714) 581-9240

APPLE COMPUTER
1 Infinity Loop
Cupertino, CA 95014
(800) 776-2333 for general information
(800) 909-0260 for a local Newton representative
(800) 538-9696 for a local Apple representative

AST RESEARCH
16215 Alton Pkwy.
Irvine, CA 92718-3616
(714) 727-4141
Fax: (714) 727-9355

COMPAQ COMPUTER CORP.
20555 State Hwy. 249
Houston, TX 77070
(800) 345-1518, (713) 370-0670
Fax: (713) 378-1442

DELL COMPUTER
1909 W. Breaker Ln.
Austin, TX 78758
(512) 338-4400
Fax: (512) 728-3653

DIGITAL EQUIPMENT
111 Powdermill Rd.
Maynard, MA 01754
(800) 344-4825, (508) 493-5111

EPSON AMERICA
20770 Madrona Ave.
P.O. Box 2903
Torrance, CA 90509
(800) 289-3776, (800) 922-8911, (310) 782-0770

IBM
Old Orchard Rd.
Armonk, NY 10504
(800) 426-3333, (800) 426-3395, (914) 766-1900

NEC TECHNOLOGIES
1255 Michael Dr.
Wood Dale, IL 60191
(800) 388-8888, (708) 860-9500

NEXT
900 Chesapeake Dr.
Redwood City, CA 94063
(415) 366-0900, (415) 780-3714

SEIKO INSTRUMENTS
1130 Ringwood Ct.
San Jose, CA 95131
(800) 888-0817, (408) 922-5800

SUN MICROSYSTEMS
2550 Garcia Ave.
Mountainview, CA 94043
(800) 786-7638, (415) 960-1300

TEXAS INSTRUMENTS
5701 Airport Rd.
Temple, TX 76502
(800) 527-3500, (817) 771-5856

TOSHIBA AMERICA INFORMATION SYSTEMS, INC.
9740 Irvine Blvd.
Irvine, CA 92718-1697
(800) 334-3445 for operator-directed calls
(800) 999-4273 for touch-tone directed calls
(714) 583-3000

XANTÉ CORP.
2559 Emogene St.
Mobile, AL 36606
(800) 926-8839, (334) 476-8189

ZENITH DATA SYSTEMS
2150 E. Lake Cook Rd.
Buffalo Grove, IL 60089
(708) 808-5000, (708) 808-4300
Fax: (708) 808-4434

PRINTER MANUFACTURERS

APPLE COMPUTER
1 Infinity Loop
Cupertino, CA 95014
(800) 776-2333 for general information
(800) 538-9696 for a local Apple representative

EPSON AMERICA
20770 Madrona Ave.
P.O. Box 2903
Torrance, CA 90509
(800) 289-3776, (800) 922-8911, (310) 782-0770

HEWLETT-PACKARD
5301 Stevens Creek Blvd.
Santa Clara, CA 95052
(800) 722-6538, (408) 246-4300

KYOCERA ELECTRONICS
100 Randolph Rd.
Somerset, NJ 08875
(908) 560-3400
Fax: (908) 560-8380

LASERMASTER
7156 Shady Oak Rd.
Eden Prairie, MN 55344
(800) 950-6868, (612) 944-9330

NEWGEN SYSTEMS
17550 Newhope St.
Fountain Valley, CA 92708
(800) 756-0556, (714) 641-8600
Fax: (714) 436-5189

QMS, INC.
1 Magnum Pass
Mobile, AL 36618
(800) 762-8894 (U.S.), (334) 633-4300
Fax: (800) 633-7213 (U.S.)
Fax: (800) 263-5508 (Canada)

RICOH IMAGING PERIPHERAL PRODUCTS
3001 Orchard Pkwy.
San Jose, CA 95134
(800) 955-3453, (408) 432-8800

SEIKO INSTRUMENTS
1130 Ringwood Ct.
San Jose, CA 95131
(800) 888-0817, (408) 922-5800

SHARP ELECTRONICS
Customer Information Center
Sharp Plaza
Mahwah, NJ 07430
(800) 237-4277

The 800 number listed above can be used to access the Sharp office nearest you. (The address is for one Sharp location of several.)

MONITOR MANUFACTURERS

APPLE COMPUTER
1 Infinity Loop
Cupertino, CA 95014
(800) 776-2333 for general information
(800) 538-9696 for a local Apple representative

BARCO, INC.
1000 Cobb Place Blvd.
Kennesaw, GA 30144
(404) 590-7900
Fax: (404) 590-8836

MAG INNOVISION
2801 S. Yale
Santa Ana, CA 92704
(800) 827-3998, (714) 751-2008

MIRROR TECHNOLOGIES, INC.
5198 W. 76th St.
Edine, MN 55439
(800) 654-5294, (612) 832-5406

MITSUBISHI ELECTRONICS AMERICA, INC.
5665 Plaza Dr.
Cypress, CA 90630
(800) 843-2515, (800) 344-6352

NANAO
23535 Kellog Ave.
Torrance, CA 90505
(800) 800-5202, (310) 325-5202

NEC TECHNOLOGIES
1255 Michael Dr.
Wood Dale, IL 60191
(800) 388-8888, (708) 860-9500

RADIUS
215 Moffett Park Dr.
Sunnyvale, CA 94089
(800) 227-2795, (408) 541-6100
(408) 541-5000 (technical support)
(800) 966-7360 (literature)

SONY
3300 Zanker Rd.
San Jose, CA 95134
(408) 432-0190
(800) 955-5505 (literature)

VIEWSONIC
12130 Mora Dr.
Santa Fe Springs, CA 90670
(800) 888-8583, (909) 869-7976
Fax: (909) 869-7958

VISIONMASTER
650 Louis Dr., Ste. 120
Warminster, PA 18974
(800) 303-IDEK, (215) 957-6543
Fax: (215) 957-6551

SCANNER MANUFACTURERS

A4TECH
717 Brea Canyon, Ste. 12
Walnut, CA 91789
(800) 760-9888, (909) 468-0071

ADVANCED NETWORK SYSTEMS
16275 Monteray Rd., Ste. N
Walnut Creek, CA 95037
(510) 947-5409

AGFA DIVISION, MILES INC.
90 Industrial Way
Wilmington, MA 01887
(800) 685-4271, (800) 343-1237

APPLE COMPUTER
1 Infinity Loop
Cupertino, CA 95014
(800) 776-2333 for general information
(800) 538-9696 for a local Apple representative

CAERE CORP.
100 Cooper Ct.
Los Gatos, CA 95030
(800) 535-7226, (408) 395-7000

CANON COMPUTER SYSTEMS, INC.
2995 Redhill Ave.
Costa Mesa, CA 92626
(800) 423-2366, (714) 438-3000

DPI ELECTRONIC IMAGING
629 Old State Rte. 74, Ste. 1
Cincinnati, OH 45244
(800) 597-3837, (513) 528-8668

EASTMAN KODAK CO.
343 State St., Dept. 841
Rochester, NY 14650-0811
(800) 242-2424, (716) 724-4000

ENVISIONS SOLUTIONS TECHNOLOGY
822 Mahler Rd.
Burlingame, CA 94010
(800) 365-7226, (415) 692-9061

EPSON AMERICA
20770 Madrona Ave.
P.O. Box 2903
Torrance, CA 90509
(800) 289-3776, (800) 922-8911, (310) 782-0770

FUJITSU
2904 Orchard Pkwy.
San Jose, CA 95134
(800) 626-4686, (408) 894-3950

HEWLETT-PACKARD
5301 Stevens Creek Blvd.
Santa Clara, CA 95052
(800) 722-6538, (800) 752-0900, (408) 246-4300

HOWTEK, INC.
21 Park Ave.
Hudson, NH 03051
(800) 444-6983, (603) 882-5200

ICG IMAGING
113 Main St.
Hackenstown, NJ 07840
(908) 813-3101

LACIE
8700 SW Creekside Pl.
Beaverton, OR 97008
(800) 999-0143, (503) 520-9000

LASERGRAPHICS, INC.
20 Ada
Irvine, CA 92718
(800) 727-2655, (714) 753-8282

LEAF SYSTEMS, INC.
250 Turnpike Rd.
Southboro, MA 01772
(800) 685-9462, (508) 460-8300

LIGHTSOURCE
17 E. Sir Francis Drake Blvd., Ste. 100
Larkspur, CA 94939
(415) 925-4200, (415) 461-8000
Fax: (415) 461-8011

LOGITECH
6505 Kaiser Dr.
Freemont, CA 94555
(800) 231-7717, (510) 795-8500

MICROTEK
3715 Doolittle Dr.
Redondo Beach, CA 90278
(800) 654-4160, (310) 352-3300

MIRROR
5198 W. 76th St.
Edine, MN 55439
(800) 654-5294, (612) 832-5406

NIKON
1300 Walt Whitman Rd.
Melville, NY 11747
(800) 526-4566, (516) 547-4200

OPTRONICS
7 Stuart Rd.
Chelmsford, MA 01824
(508) 256-4511
Fax: (508) 256-1872

PANASONIC
1 Panasonic Way
Secaucus, NJ 07094
(800) 742-8086, (708) 468-4308

PIXELCRAFT, INC.
130 Doolittle Dr., #19
San Leandro, CA 94577
(800) 933-0330, (510) 562-2480

POLAROID
784 Memorial Dr.
Cambridge, MA 02139
(800) 343-5000, (617) 386-2000

RELISYS
919 Hanson Ct.
Milpitas, CA 95035
(800) 945-0900, (408) 934-0995

RICOH IMAGING PERIPHERAL PRODUCTS
3001 Orchard Pkwy.
San Jose, CA 95134
(800) 955-3453, (408) 432-8800

SCREEN USA
5110 Tollview Dr.
Rolling Meadows, IL 60008
(708) 870-7400

SEIKO INSTRUMENTS
1130 Ringwood Ct.
San Jose, CA 95131
(800) 888-0817, (408) 922-5800

SHARP ELECTRONICS
Customer Information Center
Sharp Plaza
Mahwah, NJ 07430
(800) 237-4277

The 800 number listed above can be used to access the Sharp office nearest you. (The address is for one Sharp location of several.)

SPARK INTERNATIONAL, INC.
P.O. Box 314
Glenview, IL 60025
(708) 998-6640, (708) 998-8840

SUMMAGRAPHICS
8500 Cameron Rd.
Austin, TX 78759
(800) 337-8662, (512) 835-0900

TAMARACK
1544 Centre Pointe Dr.
Milpitas, CA 95035
(800) 643-0666, (408) 956-0144

UMAX TECHNOLOGIES, INC.
3353 Gateway Blvd.
Fremont, CA 94538
(800) 562-0311, (510) 651-8883, (510) 651-3710

VISIONSHAPE
1434 W. Taft
Orange, CA 92665
(714) 282-2668
Fax: (714) 282-2673

WACOM
501 SE Columbia Shores Blvd., Ste. 300
Vancouver, WA 98661
(800) 922-6613, (206) 750-8882

OTHER

APS TECHNOLOGIES
6131 Deramus
Kansas City, MO 64120
(816) 483-1600
Fax: (816) 483-3077

Specializes in peripheral equipment.

CALCOMP
2411 W. La Palma Dr.
P.O. Box 3250
Anaheim, CA 92803
(800) 932-1212, (714) 821-2000

Digitizing tablets.

CONNECTIX
2600 Campus Dr., Ste. 100
San Mateo, CA 94403
(800) 950-5880, (415) 513-6510
Fax: (415) 571-5195

Makes digital video camera for the Mac.

SEIKO INSTRUMENTS
1130 Ringwood Ct.
San Jose, CA 95131
(800) 888-0817, (408) 922-5800

Makes digitizing tablets.

SHREVE SYSTEMS
1200 Marshall St.
Shreveport, LA 71101
(800) 227-3971, (318) 424-9791
Fax: (318) 424-9771

Mail order source for used Macintosh computers, parts and peripherals including printers, monitors and external drives.

TECHWORKS
4030 W. Braker Ln.
Austin, TX 78759-5319
(800) 631-3918, (512) 794-8533
Fax: (512) 794-8520

Manufactures memory upgrade kits and video accelerators for PCs and laptop computers.

WACOM
501 SE Columbia Shores Blvd., Ste. 300
Vancouver, WA 98661
(800) 922-6613, (206) 750-8882

Digitizing tablets.

SOFTWARE AND COMPUTER EQUIPMENT MAIL HOUSES

Many of the computers, computer-related products and software listed elsewhere in this book can be ordered from these distributors. Call these companies for their catalogs.

APS TECHNOLOGIES
6131 Deramus
P.O. Box 4987
Kansas City, MO 64120-0087
(800) 354-1213, (816) 483-1600
Fax: (816) 483-3077

External drives, modems, cables and other peripherals as well as software. For Mac and PC.

COMPUTER DISCOUNT WAREHOUSE
1020 E. Lake Cook Rd.
Buffalo Grove, IL 60089
(800) 584-4CDW, (708) 465-6500 (technical support)

Macintosh and Apple computers and peripheral products at discount prices. Also stocks software.

DARTEK
Dept. 976
949 Larch Ave.
Elmhurst, IL 60126
(800) 832-7835, (708) 832-2100
Fax: (708) 941-1106

Software and accessories for Macintosh and PCs. Also offers discs, printers, technician's tools, storage and furniture.

DTP DIRECT
5198 W. 76th St.
Edina, MN 55439
(800) 643-0629
Fax: (612) 832-0052

Catalog offers desktop publishing software for Mac and PC. Includes a wide range of software and hardware including printers and scanners.

EGGHEAD SOFTWARE
22011 SE 51st St.
Issaquah, WA 98027-7299
(800) 669-9997
Fax: (800) 697-3447

Business and graphics applications for Mac and PCs. Also offers printers and scanners.

HIGHSMITH, INC.
W5527 Hwy. 106
P.O. Box 800
Fort Atkinson, WI 53538-0800
(800) 558-3899
Fax: (800) 835-2329

Multimedia equipment and supplies, including cameras, software, CD-ROM drives and all kinds of presentation equipment.

IMAGE CLUB GRAPHICS, INC.
729 24th Ave. SE
Calgary, Alberta T2G 5K8
Canada
(800) 661-9410
Fax: (403) 261-7013

Offers PC and Macintosh software specifically for graphic design and imaging. Includes clip files and computer fonts on floppy disk and CD-ROM. Catalog also includes design tips.

MACWAREHOUSE
47 Water St.
Norwalk, CT 06854-9958
(800) 622-6222 (U.S. orders)
(800) 925-6227 (Customer service)

Catalog of over 150 pages offers all kinds of hardware, software and other computer-related products. Special section for graphic design.

THE MAC ZONE
15815 SE 37th St.
Bellevue, WA 98006-1800
(800) 248-0800
Fax: (206) 603-2500

Catalog of over one hundred pages offers everything computer-related from cables to scanners. Offers major graphics and illustration programs, fonts and clip art on disc as well as business and game software.

PRECISION TYPE REFERENCE GUIDE
47 Mall Dr.
Commack, NY 11725-5703
(800) 248-3668, (516) 864-0167
Fax: (516) 543-5721

Offers digital fonts from major font manufacturers (indexed by font family) as well as a wide range of picture fonts. Also carries font-related software and books on typographic design and production.

3 SIXTY
Voyager
1 Bridge St.
Irvington, NY 10533
(800) 446-2001
Fax: (914) 591-6481

Catalog of multimedia presentations on CD-ROM. Selections range from entertaining to informative. Offerings include titles for adults such as Art Spiegelman's *The Complete Maus*, and many interactive titles for children.

TIGER SOFTWARE
9100 S. Dadeland Blvd., Ste. 1200
Miami, FL 33156-7816
Mac: (800) 777-2562
PC: (800) 888-4437
Fax: (305) 529-2990

PC- and Macintosh-compatible software and accessories.

BUSINESS SOFTWARE

For managing the day-in and day-out operations of your business, these programs have been developed specifically to help graphic arts professionals track and bill their projects and produce marketing and business plans.

CLIENTS & PROFITS
Working Computer
4755 Oceanside Blvd., Ste. 200
Oceanside, CA 92056
(619) 945-4334
Fax: (619) 945-2365

Job tracking, costing, billing and accounting software for the Macintosh.

DESIGNSOFT
The Design Soft Co.
P.O. Box 1130
Wheaton, IL 60189
(708) 858-5363
Fax: (708) 858-5393

Designer's job billing software for Mac and PC.

QUICKBOOKS
Intuit
2050 E. Elvira St., Ste. 100
Tucson, AZ 85706-7123
(800) 781-6999, (520) 295-3000
Fax: (520) 295-3200

Mac-compatible bookkeeping software from the makers of Quicken. Includes payroll, invoicing, accounts receivable and check writing.

SALES & MARKETING SUCCESS
180 Newport Center Dr.
Newport Beach, CA 92660
(800) 543-7788, (714) 720-8462

PC-compatible software that aids in producing a marketing plan.

SILENTPARTNER
Medi Group
180 Black Rock Rd.
Oaks, PA 19456
(610) 666-1955
Fax: (610) 666-5911

Job tracking, scheduling and accounting software for creative professionals. Mac and PC compatible.

SUCCESS
180 Newport Center Dr.
Newport Beach, CA 92660
(800) 543-7788, (714) 720-8462

PC-compatible software that aids in producing a business plan.

TIME ADVISOR
Time Advice Group
308 3rd St.
Alexandria, VA 22214
(800) 9 HELP-US
Fax: (703) 836-6453

Mac-compatible time collection and reporting software.

ILLUSTRATION

Chapter

ILLUSTRATORS

AND

ILLUSTRATION

(INCLUDING

COPYRIGHT-FREE

ILLUSTRATION)

CREATIVE DIRECTORIES

When searching for location photographers or stock agencies, don't overlook the local talent directories that many cities offer. There are also national talent books—huge directories that are regarded as the "Who's Who" of U.S. photography, illustration and design. Because they feature full-page, full-color ads of photographers' and photo agencies' work, each directory is a virtual catalog of photographic samples, offering pages and pages of styles and looks from which to choose. These directories are distributed free of charge to recognized advertising agencies, design studios and magazine publishers. They can also be purchased at art supply stores.

AMERICAN SHOWCASE ILLUSTRATION

915 Broadway, 14th Fl.
New York, NY 10010
(800) 894-7469, (212) 673-6600
Fax: (212) 673-9795

Consists of two volumes: one features illustrators' reps, the other features independent freelancers. Includes more than forty-five hundred images. Also publishes *Creative Options for Business and Annual Reports*, a directory that contains more than 150 images representing illustrators who do business-oriented work, and *Virtual Portfolio*, a directory of illustrators on CD-ROM.

THE CREATIVE ILLUSTRATION BOOK

10 Astor Pl., 6th Fl.
New York, NY 10003
(212) 539-9800
Fax: (212) 539-9801

Includes images from over four hundred illustrators.

RSVP

P.O. Box 314
Brooklyn, NY 11205
(718) 857-9267
Fax: (718) 783-2376

Publishes an annual directory consisting of two sections: illustration and design.

THE WORKBOOK

940 N. Highland Ave.
Los Angeles, CA 90038
(800) 547-2688, (213) 856-0008
Fax: (213) 856-4368

Lists thousands of illustrators in the *Illustration Portfolio*, one of four volumes of *The Workbook*. Also has alphabetical listings of studios (by region) and a four-color section with visual representations. Directory volume also lists artists reps.

STOCK ILLUSTRATION AGENCIES

The following agencies offer illustrative or other non-photographic images on a per-usage basis. If you're looking for an illustration and don't have time to commission one, call one of these agencies, tell them what subject matter, medium and style you want, and they will call, fax or send you a description or preview of the images they have that meet your requirements. Work is usually furnished in transparency format or as digital art. Most of these agencies also offer a catalog or description of available images.

ANATOMY WORKS

232 Madison Ave.
New York, NY 10016
(212) 679-8480
Fax: (212) 532-1934

Specializes in medical subject matter, including anatomy.

C.S.A. ARCHIVES

30 N. 1st St., 4th Fl.
Minneapolis, MN 55401
(612) 339-5181
Fax: (612) 339-3282

Compiled by designer Charles Spencer Anderson, this collection is primarily comprised of over forty thousand line art images from the 1920s through the 1960s. Images are some of those done by Anderson and his staff in the course of developing their projects; also includes some original images from the firm. Catalog of nonreproduceable images is $49.95. Usage fees for images vary depending on application.

CULVER PICTURES

150 W. 22nd St., Ste. 300
New York, NY 10011
(212) 645-1672
Fax: (212) 627-9112

Specializes in historical images predating the 1950s.

CUSTOM MEDICAL STOCK PHOTO
3821 N. Southport Ave.
Chicago, IL 60613
(800) 373-2677, (312) 248-3200
Fax: (312) 248-7427

Stocks millions of illustrations dealing with scientific subject matter, especially medicine, psychology and chemistry. Offers an electronic bulletin board where images can be previewed on-line. Will also supply images on CD-ROM.

IMAGE BANK
111 5th Ave.
New York, NY 10003
(800) 842-4624, (212) 529-6700
Fax: (212) 529-7024

Offers thousands of illustrations in a variety of media and styles, many by nationally known artists.

LAUGHING STOCK
192 Southville Rd.
Southborough, MA 01772
(508) 460-6058
Fax: (same)

Carries black-and-white and color illustrations from Ellwood Smith, Guy Billout and about thirty-five more nationally recognized, contemporary artists. Specializes in lighthearted subject matter.

THE STOCK ILLUSTRATION SOURCE
5 E. 16th St., 11th Fl.
New York, NY 10003
(212) 691-6400
Fax: (212) 691-6609

Offers illustrations covering a broad range of subject matter and styles. Stocks both color and black-and-white from hundreds of illustrators, many of whom are nationally recognized artists. Collection includes over seven thousand images.

THE STOCK MARKET
360 Park Ave. S., 16th Fl.
New York, NY 10010
(800) 999-0800, (212) 684-7878
Fax: (800) 283-0808

Thousands of black-and-white and color images covering all types of subject matter and media.

STOCKWORKS
11936 W. Jefferson Blvd., Ste. C
Culver City, CA 90230
(310) 390-9744
Fax: (310) 390-3161

Offers contemporary images covering all types of subject matter in color and black-and-white.

SUPERSTOCK INTERNATIONAL
7660 Centurion Pkwy.
Jacksonville, FL 32256
(800) 828-4545, (904) 565-0066
Fax: (904) 641-4480

This contemporary illustration by Tim Lewis is one of many images by well-known artists offered by Laughing Stock.

SuperStock, best-known as a stock agency for photos, also stocks illustrations.

ARTISTS' REPS

These companies represent a variety of illustrators and letterers. Call them for a catalog of artists' samples.

AMERICAN ARTISTS
353 W. 53rd St., Ste. 1W
New York, NY 10019
(212) 682-2462
Fax: (212) 582-0090

CAROLYN POTTS & ASSOCIATES
4 E. Ohio, Ste. 11
Chicago, IL 60611
(312) 944-1130
Fax: (312) 988-4236

FAMOUS FRAMES
5183 Overland Ave., #A
Culver City, CA 90230
(310) 558-3325
Fax: (310) 558-4193

FRANCE ALINE, INC.
1076 S. Ogden Dr.
Los Angeles, CA 90019
(213) 933-2500
Fax: (213) 933-2081

FREDA SCOTT
244 9th St.
San Francisco, CA 94103
(415) 621-2992
Fax: (415) 621-5202

JAMES CONRAD
2149 Lyn, #5
San Francisco, CA 94115
(415) 921-7140
Fax: (415) 921-3939

JERRY LEFF ASSOCIATES
420 Lexington Ave.
New York, NY 10170
(212) 697-8525
Fax: (212) 949-1843

JOEL HARLIB & ASSOCIATES
405 N. Wabash Ave.
Chicago, IL 60611
(312) 329-1370
Fax: (312) 329-1397

MARTHA PRODUCTIONS
4445 Overland Ave.
Culver City, CA 90230
(310) 204-1771
Fax: (310) 390-3161

MENDOLA LTD.
420 Lexington Ave.
New York, NY 10170
(212) 986-5680
Fax: (212) 818-1246

NANCY GEORGE
302 N. La Brea Ave., #116
Los Angeles, CA 90036
(213) 655-0998

PAT HACKETT
101 Yesler, #502
Seattle, WA 98104
(206) 447-1600
Fax: (206) 447-0739

RITA MARIE & FRIENDS
1464 Linden Ave.
Highland Park, IL 60035
(312) 222-0337
Fax: (312) 883-0375

SCOTT HULL & ASSOCIATES
68 E. Franklin St.
Dayton, OH 45459
(513) 433-8383
Fax: (513) 433-0434

SHARON DODGE & ASSOCIATES
3033 13th Ave., W.
Seattle, WA 98119
(206) 284-4701
Fax: (206) 622-7041

VICKI PRENTICE ASSOCIATES
1888 Century Park E., Ste. 1900
New York, NY 90667
(212) 674-4535
Fax: (212) 674-4042

WOODY COLEMAN PRESENTS
490 Rockside Rd.
Cleveland, OH 44131
(216) 661-4222
Fax: (216) 661-2879

If you're looking for free art, keep in mind that any work that has been in the public domain for over fifty years qualifies. This means that illustrations you find in very old magazines, encyclopedias, textbooks, almanacs and other literature can be used in your work as freely as clip art.

Think of the possibilities for making use of nostalgic images when browsing yard sales, flea markets and places where you can buy dated publications. The only restriction on what you select is its reproduceability—images must be clean and damage-free. The larger the image, the better the reproduction possibilities.

CLIP ART BOOKS AND SERVICES

Clip art houses commission illustrations that they sell as copyright-free art. You can use these images "as is" or as a starting point, scanning them into your computer and altering them in any way you wish.

The following is a list of firms that specialize in hardcopy clip art. Also referred to as "slicks" or "camera-ready originals," they are reproduced in books, sheets or by other tangible means, as opposed to digital clip art, which is supplied electronically. (A listing of digital clip art sources follows this listing.)

THE ART DIRECTOR'S LIBRARY
10 E. 39th St.
New York, NY 10016
(212) 889-6500
Fax: (212) 889-5504

Clip art books of vintage illustrations. Categorized into collections of old engravings and composites, the illustrations of Ron Yablon, design elements and quaint cuts.

CLIPPER
Dynamic Graphics
6000 N. Forest Park Dr.
P.O. Box 1901
Peoria, IL 61614
(800) 255-8800, (309) 688-8800
Fax: (309) 688-5873

Offers yearly or monthly subscription service to the *Clipper*, monthy books of clip art. Provides file binders, layout ideas and timely seasonal art. Cost is $38.85 monthly.

DOVER PUBLICATIONS, INC.
31 E. 2nd St.
Mineola, NY 11501
(516) 294-7000

Dover offers over one hundred books depicting anything and everything—silhouettes, vintage art, Victorian cuts, reproductions of old *Sears-Roebuck* and *Montgomery Ward* catalogs, clip art alphabets, trademarks and symbols.

GRAPHIC SOURCE CLIP ART LIBRARY
Graphic Products Corp.
1480 S. Wolf Rd.
Wheeling, IL 60090-6514
(708) 537-9300

Offers over sixty books in many styles on a variety of subjects. Each book contains at least one hundred illustrations. The company sells most of its books through art supply stores, but orders of $25 or more are accepted.

NORTH LIGHT BOOKS
1507 Dana Ave.
Cincinnati, OH 45207
(800) 289-0963, (513) 531-2690

Offers twenty-four books covering various subjects, including holidays, animals, food and drink, sports, men, women, couples, families, borders, backgrounds, patterns, textures and spot illustrations. Each book is $6.99 and contains at least one hundred illustrations. Also publishes *Pictograms & Typefaces of the World* and *Trademarks & Symbols of the World*.

DIGITAL CLIP ART SOURCES

Companies offering digital clip art commission illustrations that they digitize and sell as copyright-free art. These images are already in electronic format, meaning they can be brought into your computer, sized, altered and manipulated to your heart's content, or used as-is.

If you work on a computer but you don't own a scanner, digital clip art is a great source of pre-scanned artwork. If you have a scanner, pre-scanned images will still save you scanning time and supply you with the cleanest possible images, at a resolution and size that will work best for you. When calling the following companies, check to see if their collections are compatible with your computer and software.

Mad Boss   3.5" Disk 2   Knife   Mac   Hitchhiking Exec   File Cabinet

Art Parts offers digital clip art with a contemporary, woodcut look. The company offers collections covering a variety of subjects on CD-ROM. See Art Parts' listing at right for further information.

ARROGLYPHS

Arro International
P.O. Box 167
Montclair, NJ 07042
(800) 243-1515
Fax: (201) 509-0728

Library includes black-and-white and color images. Individual collections consist of energy-related images, wildlife, recycling, living planet images and pollution. Volumes of fifty-plus images are $69 each.

ART PARTS

P.O. Box 2926
Orange, CA 92669-0926
(714) 771-6754
Fax: (714) 633-9617

Original illustrations with contemporary flair, offering a variety of subject matter rendered in woodcut style. Offers twenty-seven sets organized by subject. Each CD-ROM collection contains thirteen sets or over 850 illustrations total.

ARTS & LETTERS

5926 Midway Rd.
Dallas, TX 75244
(214) 661-8960

Offers Arts & Letters Express, a library of over ten thousand images that come installed on the company's software. Available on CD-ROM for $99.95. Set of ninty-five floppies is $124.95.

BACKGROUNDS AND BORDERS

Letraset USA
40 Eisenhower Dr.
Paramus, NJ 07653
(800) 526-9073
Fax: (201) 845-5047

Consists of six collections of high- and low-resolution versions of clouds, waterdrops, nature scenes, geometric patterns, etc. Comes on six disks with twelve to fifteen images per disk.

CLICKART EPS ILLUSTRATIONS

T/Maker Co.
1390 Villa St.
Mountain View, CA 94041
(800) 986-2537, (415) 962-0195
Fax: (415) 962-0201

Offers many different collections of line art on floppy disk and CD-ROM. Individual collections focus on cartoons, church bulletin and newsletter images, holidays, business, real estate and Christian holidays. Number of images varies per collection. Prices range from $19.95 to $59.95. Also offers a special package, the Incredible Image Pack, which contains two thousand images for $49.95.

CLIPPER

Dynamic Graphics
6000 N. Forest Park Dr.
P.O. Box 1901
Peoria, IL 61614
(800) 255-8800, (309) 688-8800
Fax: (309) 688-5873

Monthly clip subscription service on CD-ROM. Provides a different disc every month with eighty-five to one hundred black-and-white illustrations, including timely seasonal art. Cost is $70.85 per month.

COREL GALLERY

1600 Carling Ave.
Ottawa, Ontario K1Z 8R7
Canada
(800) 772-6735, (613) 728-3733
Fax: (613) 761-9176

Offers ten thousand PICT format clip art images on CD-ROM. Collection includes over fifty image categories, including business, maps, food, transporation and celebrities. Cost is $59.

DESIGNER CLIPART

Micrografx, Inc.
1303 Arapaho Rd.
Richardson, TX 75081
(800) 272-3729
Fax: (214) 994-6475

Collection consists of the following libraries: general subject matter, business, technical symbols, U.S. maps and world maps. Each library consists of about one thousand line art images and sells for $49.95.

DESKTOP ART

Dynamic Graphics
6000 N. Forest Park Dr.
Peoria, IL 61614
(800) 255-8800, (309) 688-8800
Fax: (309) 688-5873

Offers monthly clip subscription service on CD-ROM or diskette. Provides a different set of black-and-white illustrations every month, including timely seasonal art. Cost is $52.50 per month for fifty-six images.

DIGICLIPS

U-Design, Inc.
201 Ann St.
Hartford, CT 06102
(203) 278-3648

Offers four clip libraries, each consisting of two hundred line art illustrations on diskette. Images consist of vintage and contemporary art depicting social situations, food, political cartoons and more. Cost is $59.95 for all four disks.

EXPRESIV COLLECTION

Tiger Software
9100 S. Dadeland Blvd., Ste. 1200
Miami, FL 33156-7816
Mac: (800) 777-2562
PC: (800) 888-4437
Fax: (305) 529-2990

Three libraries: color and black-and-white illustrations, maps and borders on PC- or Mac-compatible diskette or CD-ROM.

IMAGE CLUB GRAPHICS, INC.

729 24th Ave. SE
Calgary, Alberta T2G 5K8
Canada
(800) 661-9410, (403) 262-8008
Fax: (403) 261-7013

Offers thirty-four different volumes on CD-ROM and floppy disk. Black-and-white line art and continuous-tone collections, organized by subject matter and illustration style.

LETRASET LIBRARY

Letraset USA
40 Eisenhower Dr.
Paramus, NJ 07653
(800) 526-9073
Fax: (201) 845-5047

Offers decorative borders, initials, advertising motifs, and other images and symbols from Letraset's dry transfer library. Consists of four collections of 150 images each, organized by subject on floppy

---

There are a lot of companies offering digital clip art collections. Because so many have just come on the market, it's hard to determine which collections offer images that will work best for your publication needs. When checking out the image collections offered in this section keep these considerations in mind:

- *Compatibility—In addition to PC vs. Mac platforms, be sure images will work with the software you're using.*
- *Format—Formats include EPS, TIFF, PICT, GCM and WMF. Determine whether the image formats in a given collection will offer the versatility you need for your design applications.*
- *Vector vs. PostScript—Vector-based images can be enlarged without losing clarity or developing a pixelated look.*

disk or CD-ROM. Available off-the-shelf at retailers of art and design supplies.

METRO IMAGEBASE ELECTRONIC ART

18723 Ventura Blvd., Ste. 210
Tarzana, CA 91256
(800) 525-1552

Collection consists of twenty-three titles on diskette. Each title focuses on a subject area or period style such as sports, health and art deco images. Also offers two CD-ROM collections: General subject matter and food. Images are color and black-and-white. For best price, order from the Mac-WAREHOUSE (contact information is in chapter one, page 13).

PRO 3000 AND EURO 5000

Tiger Software
9100 S. Dadeland Blvd., Ste. 1200
Miami, FL 33156-7816
(800) 848-9531
Mac: (800) 777-2562
PC: (800) 888-4437
Fax: (305) 529-2990

Features a collection of images from European artists. Images consist of black-and-white and color line art of embellishments, maps, universal symbols, holiday motifs and more. Each collection consists of about four thousand images on CD-ROM. Cost is $59.90 each or $89.90 for two.

TOTEM GRAPHICS

5109-A Capitol Blvd.
Tumwater, WA 98501
(206) 352-1851
Fax: (206) 352-2554

Offers over seventeen hundred images on CD-ROM (over twenty different subject titles). Also offers a collection of police and firefighting images on diskette.

"Whirligig," an illustration font offered by Emigre Graphics, offers limitless possibilities for creating borders and patterns, such as the one shown here. The font was designed by Zuzana Licko. See Emigre's listing at right for more information.

being marketed as picture fonts—images which are accessible as keystrokes.

Picture fonts offer the same line-art reproduction possibilities as any clip art images. They can also ensure clarity at a larger size, because they are scaled by changing their point size, as you would when sizing any font on your computer. The following companies offer keyboard-accessible illustrations:

EMIGRE

4475 D St.

Sacramento, CA 95819

(800) 944-9021, (916) 451-4344

Fax: (916) 451-4351

Offers original illustrations by avant-garde designers. Includes a variety of styles and subject matter including borders and graphic ornaments.

FONTEK DESIGN FONTS

Letraset USA

40 Eisenhower Dr.

Paramus, NJ 07653

(800) 526-9073

Fax: (201) 845-5047

Original illustrations organized by subject matter and illustrative styles. Includes primitive and retro looks, wildlife images and embellishments. Eighteen diskettes offered, with approximately seventy images per diskette. Available off-the-shelf at retailers of art and design supplies.

PICTURE FONTS

℅ Fonthaus

15 Perry Ave., A7

Norwalk, CT 06850

(800) 942-9110

Collection consists of a wide range of images, organized by style and subject matter. Illustration styles vary considerably and include primitive looks, as well as contemporary and vintage.

YOUTH SPECIALTIES

P.O. Box 4406

Spartanburg, SC 29305-4406

(800) 776-8008

Fax: (803) 583-7381

Offers six volumes of line art images at $49.95 each. Collections of illustrations are organized into borders and symbols, phrases and verses, spiritual matter, general images and sports.

PRECISION TYPE

47 Mall Dr.

Commack, NY 11725-5703

(800) 248-3668, (516) 864-0167

Fax: (516) 543-5721

Offers a variety of symbol fonts from different designers and font manufacturers. Subject areas include wood type ornaments, astrological signs, embellishments, warning symbols, card faces, company logos and many more.

PICTURE FONTS

If you're familiar with Zapf Dingbats, you know how easy it is to access symbols from your computer keyboard. A wide range of clip art possibilities are now

RUBBER STAMPS

To the uninitiated, rubber stamp enthusiasts are a rare breed—they have their own association, trade magazines and conventions. So what's all the excitement about? For one thing, if you browse through any of the catalogs from the manufacturers listed below you'll be impressed with the novelty of the images available. Layering, borders and pattern creation are easy with stamps—the creative possibilities are tremendous!

The companies listed here stock rubber stamps of all kinds of images as well as stamp pads and other rubber stamp supplies. In addition to mounted stamps, many of these manufacturers also offer unmounted stamps at a discount. Call or write to each for a catalog of images.

A STAMP IN THE HAND CO.
20630 S. Leapwood Ave., Ste. B
Carson, CA 90746
(310) 329-8555

Stamps with a hand-carved eraser look in a variety of designs. Also offers custom stamps. Send $3.75 for catalog.

ALL NIGHT MEDIA
454 DuBois
San Rafael, CA 94901
(415) 459-3013
Fax: (800) 503-5700

BIZARRO
P.O. Box 16160
Rumford, RI 02916
(401) 728-9560

Alphabet sets and a variety of novelty stamps. Will produce custom stamps from customer-furnished artwork. Also offers embossing powders, rainbow stamp pads and a user's guide. Will send catalog at no charge.

DELAFIELD STAMP CO.
P.O. Box 56
Delafield, WI 53018
(414) 646-8599

Over four hundred designs plus stamping accessories. Will send catalog at no charge.

DOUBLE D RUBBER STAMPS INC.
P.O. Box 1
Olivia, MN 56277
(612) 826-2288
Fax: (612) 826-2211

Over nine-hundred designs including sign language alphabet stamps. Offers catalog for $3 which is credited to purchase.

GRAPHIC RUBBER STAMP CO.
11250 Magnolia Blvd.
North Hollywood, CA 91601
(818) 762-9443
Fax: (818) 762-4251

A wide range of images as well as embossing powders, stamp pads, technique videos and paper items. Offers three different catalogs of stamp images at $2 per catalog.

GUMBO GRAPHICS
P.O. Box 11801
Eugene, OR 95440
(503) 226-9895
Fax: (503) 223-2824

Over two thousand images including unusual items, reproductions and more. Will send catalog for $2.

HAMILTON ARTS
5340 Hamilton Ave.
Cleveland, OH 44114
(800) 831-4427, (216) 431-9001
Fax: (800) 831-0029

Original hand-drawn images. Cost of catalog is $2.

Gumbo Graphics offers thousands of rubber stamps, many of them nostalgic images such as this sampling from its railroad collection. See the Gumbo Graphics listing at left for further information.

If you want to locate more outlets for rubber stamps and stamp supplies, check out Rubberstampmadness, *a bimonthly magazine for rubber stamp enthusiasts that is available from many of the outlets listed on pages 23 and 24. Or write or call:* Rubberstampmadness, *408 SW Monroe, #210, Corvallis, OR 97333; (503) 752-0075. Cost of subscription is $20 per year.*

HIPPO HEART
28 2nd Ave.
San Mateo, CA 94401
(415) 347-4477
Fax: (415) 347-4751

A variety of images including garden scenes, borders and corners. Will send catalog for $2, refundable at the time of purchase.

INKADINKADO
60 Cummings Park
Woburn, MA 01801
(800) 888-4652, (617) 938-6100
Fax: (617) 938-5585

Call for a free catalog.

JAM PAPER & ENVELOPE
111 3rd Ave.
New York, NY 10003
(212) 473-6666
Fax: (212) 473-7300

Rubber stamps made from supplied artwork plus novelty stamps. Will furnish free catalog.

L.A. STAMPWORKS
P.O. Box 2329
North Hollywood, CA 91610
(818) 761-8757
Fax: (818) 766-9679

Over one thousand images including cartoon characters in action, balloon quotes, vintage images, borders and more. Offers catalog for $5.

NAME BRAND
P.O. Box 34245
Potomac, MD 20827
(301) 299-3062
Fax: (301) 299-3063

Custom stamps as well as standard slogans: "We've Moved," "Thank-You" and more.

100 PROOF PRESS
Rte. 1, Box 136
Eaton, NY 13334
(315) 684-3547

Close to three thousand images including ethnic and vintage images, make-a-face parts and more. Cost of catalog is $4.

POSH IMPRESSIONS
30100 Town Center Dr., Ste. V
Laguna Real, CA 92621
(800) 421-POSH

Over forty thousand images plus videos and other learning aids. Offers catalog for $3.

RUBBER STAMP ZONE
777 Ridgeway, Ste. 203
Sausolito, CA 94965
(800) 993-9119

Offers thousands of images. Offers catalog for $2.

STAMP-A-BARBARA
505 Paseo Nuevo
Santa Barbara, CA 93101
(805) 962-4077
Fax: (805) 568-0330

Manufactures stamps and carries stamps from a variety of companies.

STAMP YOUR ART OUT
9725 Kenwood Rd.
Cincinnati, OH 45242-6130
(513) 793-4558
Fax: (513) 563-9620

Distribution center for stamps from a variety of manufacturers.

MANUFACTURERS OF DRY TRANSFER GRAPHICS AND SYMBOLS

These companies manufacture rub-down transfers of patterns, textures, bursts, architectural and transportation symbols, etc. These items are most commonly sold through art supply stores, but you can contact the manufacturer directly to locate a retailer in your area.

GRAPHIC PRODUCTS CORP.
1480 S. Wolf Rd.
Wheeling, IL 60090-6514
(708) 537-9300

LETRASET USA
40 Eisenhower Dr.
Paramus, NJ 07653
(800) 526-9073
Fax: (201) 845-5047

ILLUSTRATION SOFTWARE

These programs can be used to render line drawings and continuous tone images, patterns, gradations and type in black-and-white and in four color. They can also be used with digital tablets to produce rendering techniques that simulate brushstrokes.

ADOBE ILLUSTRATOR
1585 Charleston Rd.
P.O. Box 7900
Mountainview, CA 94039-7900
(800) 833-6687
(800) 235-0078 (for product literature)

ALTSYS FREEHAND
411 1st Ave., S.
Seattle, WA 98104-2871
(206) 622-5500
Fax: (206) 343-4240

CANVAS
Deneba Software
7400 SW 87th Ave.
Miami, FL 33173
(800) 733-6322, (305) 596-5644
Fax: (305) 273-9069

CORELDRAW
1600 Carling Ave.
Ottawa, Ontario K1Z 8R7
Canada
(800) 772-6735, (613) 728-3733
Fax: (613) 761-9176

MACROMEDIA FREEHAND
600 Townsend
San Francisco, CA 94103
(800) 326-2128, (415) 252-2000

PHOTOGRAPHY

Chapter

4

PHOTOGRAPHERS

AND

PHOTOGRAPHY

(INCLUDING

COPYRIGHT-FREE

PHOTOGRAPHY)

Stock photos

CD Rom

CREATIVE DIRECTORIES

When searching for location photographers or stock agencies, don't overlook the local talent directories that many cities offer. In addition, there are national talent books: huge directories that are regarded as the "Who's Who" of U.S. photography, illustration and design. Because they feature full-page, full-color ads of photographers' and photo agencies' work, each directory is a virtual catalog of photographic samples, offering pages and pages of styles and looks from which to choose.

THE CREATIVE BLACK BOOK

10 Astor Pl., 6th Fl.

New York, NY 10003

(212) 539-9800

Fax: (212) 539-9801

Directory includes examples from about three hundred photographers. Also lists stock photography agencies, photo labs and retouchers.

KLIK! SHOWCASE PHOTOGRAPHY

915 Broadway, 14th Fl.

New York, NY 10010

(800) 894-7469, (212) 673-6600

Fax: (212) 673-9795

Features more than thirteen hundred photos from photographers working in all parts of the U.S.

VIRTUAL PORTFOLIO/SHOWCASE CD

915 Broadway, 14th Fl.

New York, NY 10010

(800) 894-7469, (212) 673-6600

Fax: (212) 673-9795

Directory of photographers on CD-ROM. Published by American Showcase, it includes more than two thousand images.

THE WORKBOOK

940 N. Highland Ave.

Los Angeles, CA 90038

(800) 547-2688, (213) 856-0008

Fax: (213) 856-4368

Photography volume offers four-color representation of thousands of photographers organized alphabetically by region. Directory volume also lists retouchers, stylists, make-up artists and model agencies.

TIP

Need to find a model, photo stylist or make-up artist? In addition to photographers, many of the talent directories listed in this chapter offer listings for these and other photography-related services.

STOCK PHOTOGRAPHY ON CD-ROM

As opposed to searching for images from stock agencies, stock images on CD-ROM enable the user to immediately draw from a number of images already in digital form. Some of these photos will have a user's fee; others are copyright-free. Each of the firms listed offers photo libraries on CD-ROM or diskette. Check individual listings for image resolution and usage rights.

Take note: When contacted for a description of their offerings, most of the agencies below mentioned that they would soon be adding to their line of images on CD-ROM. When calling the companies below, you may want to ask if additional photo libraries are available.

AZTECH NEW MEDIA

1 Scarsdale Rd.

Donmills, Ontario M3B 2R2

Canada

(416) 449-4787

Fax: (416) 449-1058

Offers WorldBank Personal Stock Image Library, two collections of images on CD-ROM. One collection offers three thousand low-res (seventy-two dpi) images, suitable for multimedia, at $99.95. The other collection, retailing at $299.95, consists of three thousand high-res images (three hundred dpi). Agency also offers smaller collections of images.

BACKGROUNDS AND BORDERS

Letraset USA

40 Eisenhower Dr.

Paramus, NJ 07653

(800) 526-9073

Fax: (201) 845-5047

Consists of six collections of high- and low-resolution versions of clouds, waterdrops, nature scenes, geometric patterns, etc. Comes on six disks with twelve to fifteen images per disk.

BLACK BOOK PORTFOLIO

10 Astor Pl., 6th Fl.

New York, NY 10003

(212) 539-9800

Fax: (212) 539-9801

Offers eleven hundred low-res stock photos that can be used in comps. User pays agency a fee for high-res version. Cost is $49.

COREL PROFESSIONAL PHOTOS ON CD-ROM
1600 Carling Ave.
Ottawa, Ontario K1Z 8R7
Canada
(800) 772-6735, (613) 728-3733
Fax: (613) 761-9176

Offers twenty thousand high-res images—one hundred on each of two hundred CD-ROMs. Discs are organized by subject matter. Each disc costs $19.95.

COSMOTONE
24422 S. Main St., Ste. 503
Carson, CA 80745
(800) 995-6229, (310) 513-6069
Fax: (310) 513-6298

Offers over one thousand background images.

DIGITAL STOCK
400 S. Sierra Ave., Ste. 100
Solana Beach, CA 92075
(800) 545-4514, (619) 794-4040
Fax: (619) 794-4041

Offers an extensive library of digital images consisting of thirty different CD-ROMs, retailing for $249 or $349 apiece. Each CD-ROM collection focuses on a particular subject area and contains one hundred high-res images. An accompanying CD-ROM catalog, costing $39.95, contains low-res versions of the images in the high-res collection so that users can browse and comp with these images before buying.

EXPRESIV TEXTURES
Tiger Software
9100 S. Dadeland Blvd., Ste. 1200
Miami, FL 33156-7816
Mac: (800) 777-2562
PC: (800) 888-4437
Fax: (305) 529-2990

Disk contains sixteen different textural images that work well as background effects.

FPG INTERNATIONAL
32 Union Sq., E.
New York, NY 10003
(212) 777-4210
Fax: (212) 995-9652

Currently offers fifty-seven hundred images on CD-ROM at a cost of $175. Images are low-res versions of photos from the agency's files that offer unlimited comp useage. Users pay a usage fee if high-res originals are furnished.

THE IMAGE BANK
111 5th Ave.
New York, NY 10003
(800) 842-4624, (212) 529-6700
Fax: (212) 529-7024

Contains more than forty-one hundred images.

IMAGE CLUB GRAPHICS, INC.
729 24th Ave. SE
Calgary, Alberta T2G 5K8
Canada
(800) 661-9410, (403) 262-8008
Fax: (403) 261-7013

Offers photo libraries of isolated objects, landscapes and background images.

ISLAND PHOTO-GRAPHICS
P.O. Box 78
Langley, WA 98260
(800) 635-1069, (360) 221-3727
Fax: (360) 221-1459

Offers 121 high-resolution images of flowers on CD-ROM for $59.95.

PHOTOTONE SELECTOR
Letraset USA
40 Eisenhower Dr.
Paramus, NJ 07653
(800) 526-9073
Fax: (201) 845-5047

Two-volume set consists of 1,132 low-res background images on CD-ROM or a selector book with images that can be scanned for comps. An unlocking code allows users to access high-res versions for final output.

SAN FRANCISCO STOCK
48 Century Ln.
Petaluma, CA 94952
(800) 334-5222, (415) 397-3040
Fax: (707) 766-8811

CD-ROM library of fifteen hundred regional images from San Francisco, Northern California and the Pacific Northwest.

THE STOCK MARKET
360 Park Ave. S., 16th Fl.
New York, NY 10010
(800) 999-0800, (212) 684-7878
Fax: (800) 283-0808

Offers six thousand images on CD-ROM for $59.95. Images are low-res versions of photos from the agency's files. Users pay a usage fee when high-res originals are furnished for publication.

The Picture Agency Council of America (PACA) publishes an annual directory that includes a list of around eighty of its stock agency members, what they offer and how to contact them. The PACA Directory also includes ethical guidelines for agencies and clients. Contact them at: PACA, P.O. Box 308, Northfield, MN 55057-0308, (800) 457-PACA, Fax: (507) 645-7066.

STUDIO PRODUCTIONS
18000 E. 400 S.
Elizabethtown, IN 47232
(800) 359-2964, (513) 251-7014
Fax: (513) 861-2932

Designer's background collection consists of 104 high-res images and low-res comping versions. Includes leaves, textures and other images suitable for background effects. Cost is $249. Company also sells images for multimedia. See listing in chapter twelve on page 119.

WEATHERSTOCK
P.O. Box 31808
Tucson, AZ 85751
(520) 751-9964, (520) 751-1185

Offers one hundred high-resolution images on CD-ROM of weather-related photos for $199. Includes tornadoes, storms, clouds and some geographical shots.

WESTLIGHT
2223 S. Carmelina Ave.
Los Angeles, CA 90064
(800) 872-7872, (310) 820-7077
Fax: (310) 820-2687

Offers a CD-ROM catalog for $59.95 that includes forty-five hundred low-res images from the agency's files. Users pay a usage fee when high-res originals are furnished for publication.

SOURCES OF STOCK PHOTOGRAPHY BY REGION

Stock agencies loan photographic images to users who are charged a one-time fee for publishing these images. If you're looking for a particular photographic image, call a stock agency, tell them what you want, and they will call, fax or send you a description or preview of the images they have that meet your requirements. Photographic images are available as prints, slides, 4"×5" and larger-sized transparencies, as well as digital files. Fees will vary, depending on the image format, usage and agency research time involved. If you contract to use a specific image, in addition to paying the fee, you are responsible for returning the original to the agency in a timely manner.

The listings in this section are organized by region. Most offer images specific to their locale as well as general subject matter. Some specialize in images of a particular kind. All will respond to phone inquiries by sending a free catalog or a description of their photographic subject areas.

NEW ENGLAND (CT, NH, MA, ME, RI, VT)

CAPESCAPES
542 Higgins Corral Rd.
West Yarmouth, MA 02673
(508) 362-8222
Fax: same

Stocks close to twenty-thousand photos of seascapes, primarily of New England coastline, but also many scenes from the southern Atlantic, Gulf of Mexico and the Pacific coastline.

THE PICTURE CUBE
67 Broad St.
Boston, MA 02129
(800) 335-CUBE, (617) 443-1113
Fax: (617) 443-1114

Stocks black-and-white as well as color images. Also has vintage photos. Extensive file of regional images. Publishes catalog that also includes images from the Milwaukee-based Third Coast stock agency.

VISUALS UNLIMITED
P.O. Box 146
East Swanzey, NH 03445
Or:
50 Sawyers Crossing Rd.
West Swanzey, NH 03469
(603) 352-6436
Fax: (603) 357-7931

Offers 400,000 contemporary images, 80 percent color, encompassing work of over four hundred photographers. Large file of science and geographical images.

MID-ATLANTIC (DC, DE, MD, NJ, NY, PA)

AMTRAK CORPORATE COMMUNICATIONS
60 Massachusetts Ave., NE
Washington, DC 20002
(202) 906-3857

ANIMALS, ANIMALS ENTERPRISES
580 Broadway, Ste. 1102
New York, NY 10012
(212) 925-2110
Fax: (212) 925-2796
Or:
17 Railroad Ave.
Chatham, NY 12037
(518) 392-5500
Fax: (518) 392-5550

Specializes in nature and wildlife photography.

ART RESOURCE
65 Bleecker St.
New York, NY 10012
(212) 505-8700
Fax: (212) 420-9286

Agency accesses archival sources for photos of great art and architecture.

THE BETTMAN ARCHIVES/BETTMAN NEWSPHOTOS
902 Broadway, 5th Fl.
New York, NY 10010
(212) 777-6200
Fax: (212) 533-4034

Specializes in nostalgic and historical images. Stocks millions of photos and some illustrations. Can send preview images on-line to subscribers of PressLink and CompuServe. Also offers the Bettman Portable Archive, a book featuring six thousand black-and-white and color images (non-reproduceable) from the Bettman collection for $29.95.

BLACK STAR
116 E. 27th St.
New York, NY 10016
(212) 679-3288
Fax: (212) 447-9732

Stocks close to four million photos on mostly social issues and political subject matter. Includes historical as well as contemporary imagery. Will also send photographers on assignment.

COMSTOCK, INC.
30 Irving Pl.
New York, NY 10003
(800) 225-2727, (212) 353-3383
Fax: (212) 353-3383

Offers over five million photographs covering all types of subject matter. In addition to traditional photographic formats, will furnish digital files on disk. Can also send digital images on-line.

CULVER PICTURES, INC.
150 W. 22nd St., Ste. 300
New York, NY 10011
(212) 645-1672
Fax: (212) 627-9112

Offers close to ten million color and black-and-white images predating the 1950s. Collection includes millions of movie stills.

DUOMO PHOTOGRAPHY, INC.
133 W. 19th St.
New York, NY 10014
(212) 243-1150
Fax: (212) 633-1279

Specializes in sports photos dating from the 1960s to the present.

ESTO
222 Valley Pl.
Mamaroneck, NY 10543
(914) 698-4060
Fax: (914) 698-1033

Specializes in photos of art and architecture. Can draw from existing supply of images or send photographers on assignment.

FASHIONS IN STOCK
23-68 Steinway St.
Astoria, NY 11105
(718) 721-1373
Fax: (718) 721-1373
Or:
125 5th Ave.
New York, NY 10003
(212) 529-4372

Specializes in fashion photography from the 1940s to the present.

FOCUS ON SPORTS, INC.
222 E. 46th St., 4th Fl.
New York, NY 10017
(212) 661-6860
Fax: (212) 983-3031

Stocks sports-related subject matter dating from the 1960s to the present.

FPG INTERNATIONAL
32 Union Square, E.
New York, NY 10003
(212) 777-4210
Fax: (212) 995-9652

Stocks approximately six million images covering all types of subject matter. Also offers fifty-seven hundred images on CD-ROM (low-res versions,

$175). Offers preview images on-line through K-PEX (Kodak Picture Exchange).

FUNDAMENTAL PHOTOGRAPHS
210 Forsythe St.
New York, NY 10002
(212) 473-5770
Fax: (212) 228-5059

Science stock agency specializing in chemistry and physics photos. Collection is used primarily for textbook visuals.

GRANT HEILMAN PHOTOGRAPHY, INC.
506 W. Lincoln Ave.
Lititz, PA 17543
(800) 622-2046, (717) 626-0296
Fax: (717) 626-0971

Offers close to 400,000 images, covering all types of subject matter, including contemporary and historical. Charges no research fee.

H. ARMSTRONG ROBERTS
4203 Locust St.
Philadelphia, PA 19104
(800) 786-6300, (215) 386-6300
Fax: (800) 786-1920

In business since 1926, this agency offers an extensive file of black-and-white archival images as well as over 500,000 color images.

HAROLD M. LAMBERT STUDIOS, INC.
2801 W. Cheltenham Ave.
Philadelphia, PA 19150
(215) 224-1400

Close to one million color and black-and-white images, many historical.

THE IMAGE BANK
111 5th Ave.
New York, NY 10003
(800) 842-4624, (212) 529-6700
Fax: (212) 529-7024

Over a million images, historical as well as contemporary, black-and-white and color. In addition to photography, offers illustration and film.

INDEX STOCK PHOTOGRAPHY
126 5th Ave.
New York, NY 10011
(800) 729-7466, (212) 406-2440
Fax: (212) 633-1914

Offers close to a half million contemporary and vintage photographs covering a broad range of subject matter.

JAY MAISEL PHOTOGRAPHY
190 Bowery
New York, NY 10012
(212) 431-5013
Fax: (212) 925-6092

Over one million photographs covering a broad range of subject matter. All color and contemporary imagery.

LIAISON INTERNATIONAL
11 E. 26th St., 17th Fl.
New York, NY 10010
(800) 488-0484, (212) 447-2514
Fax: (212) 447-2534

Specializes in stock files for advertising agencies and graphic designers. Represents 225 photographers worldwide and offers over 250,000 mostly contemporary images.

MAGNUM PHOTOS
151 W. 25th St., 5th Fl.
New York, NY 10001
(212) 929-6000
Fax: (212) 929-9325

Offers millions of journalistic photos, covering a broad range of subject matter, from the 1930s to the present. Specialty is World War II photographs.

MEDICHROME
232 Madison Ave.
New York, NY 10016
(212) 679-8480
Fax: (212) 532-1934

Specializes in medical subject matter. Off-shoot of this agency, Anatomy Works, carries stock medical illustrations.

MOVIE STAR NEWS
134 W. 18th St.
New York, NY 10011
(212) 620-8160
Fax: (212) 827-0634

Offers millions of images of motion picture stars from the silent era to the present.

NATIONAL BASEBALL LIBRARY
P.O. Box 590
Cooperstown, NY 13326
(607) 547-7200, (607) 547-4094

As part of the Baseball Hall of Fame, this library offers all kinds of current and historical images relating to baseball. Collection dates back to the mid-1800s and includes some etchings as well as color and black-and-white photos.

PETER ARNOLD, INC.
1181 Broadway
New York, NY 10001
(800) 289-7468, (212) 481-1190
Fax: (212) 481-3409

Offers close to 400,000 images, mostly color. Specializes in animals, wildlife, nature, medical and scientific subject matter. Also offers travel and traditional subject matter.

PHOTO RESEARCHERS, INC.
60 E. 56th St.
New York, NY 10022
(800) 833-9033, (212) 758-3420
Fax: (212) 355-0731

Over one million color and black-and-white images. Offers an extensive file of science, nature and medical imagery.

PICTORIAL PARADE, INC.
530 W. 25th St., 6th Fl.
New York, NY 10001
(800) 688-5656, (212) 675-0115
Fax: (212) 675-0379

Offers journalistic photos and historical photos. File also includes 19th-century engravings. Can supply images on CD-ROM.

RETNA
18 E. 17th St., 3rd Fl.
New York, NY 10003
(212) 255-0622
Fax: (212) 255-1224

Specializes in celebrities, particularly pop musicians. Library includes images dating from the 1950s to the present.

THE STOCK MARKET
360 Park Ave. S., 16th Fl.
New York, NY 10010
(800) 999-0800, (212) 684-7878
Fax: (800)283-0808

Over two million images covering all types of general subject matter, mostly color. Offers some illustration.

TIME LIFE SYNDICATION
1271 6th Ave., Rm. 2858
New York, NY 10020
(212) 522-4800
Fax: (212) 522-0328

Offers primarily fashion and human interest subject matter from the archives of *Time/Life*.

TONY STONE IMAGES
475 Park Ave. S., 28th Fl.
New York, NY 10016
(800) 234-7880, (212) 545-8220
Fax: (212) 545-9797

Contemporary subject matter, mostly lifestyle and travel. Based in London, the agency also has offices in Chicago, Toronto and Los Angeles. Charges no research fee.

UNIPHOTO
19 W. 21st St., Ste. 901
New York, NY 10010
(800) 225-4060, (212) 627-4060
Fax: (212) 645-9619
Or:
3307 M St. NW, Ste. 300
Washington, DC 20007
(800) 345-0546
Fax: (202) 338-5578

Offers over three million mostly color images, dating from the late 1950s to the present.

VISIONS PHOTO AGENCY, INC.
220 W. 19th St., Ste. 500
New York, NY 10011
(212) 255-4047
Fax: (212) 691-1177

Stocks mostly travel and adventure photos. Images are all contemporary.

An image from the collection of Liaison International by photographer Richard Elkins. The stock agency represents the work of over two hundred international and domestic photographers. For more information, see Liaison International's listing on page 32.

SOUTHEAST (AL, FL, GA, KY, MS, NC, SC, TN, VA, WV)

ARMS COMMUNICATIONS
1517 Maurice Dr.
Woodbridge, VA 22191
(703) 690-3338
Fax: (703) 490-3298

Specializes in military subject matter. Collection is mostly contemporary, with some images dating back to the Vietnam era.

KULIK PHOTOGRAPHIC/MILITARY STOCK
7209 Deerfield Ct.
Falls Church, VA 22043
(703) 979-1427

Specializes in military photos dating from World War I to the present.

PHOTRI-PHOTO RESEARCH
3701 S. George Mason Dr., Ste. C2N
Falls Church, VA 22041
(800) 544-0385, (703) 931-8600
Fax: (703) 998-8407

Best known for its extensive collection of military and space-related subject matter. Also offers lifestyle, scenic and other general stock images.

SHARPSHOOTERS, INC.
4950 SW 72nd Ave., Ste. 114
Miami, FL 32155
(305) 666-1266
Fax: (305) 666-5485

Offers mostly lifestyle photography, landscapes and other contemporary imagery.

SOUTHERN STOCK PHOTOS
3601 W. Commercial Blvd., Ste. 33
Ft. Lauderdale, FL 33309
(800) 486-7118, (305) 486-7117
Fax: (305) 486-7118

Mostly general imagery. Offers extensive file of regional and Caribbean subject matter.

SUPERSTOCK
7660 Centurion Pkwy.
Jacksonville, FL 32256
(800) 828-4545, (904) 565-0066
Fax: (904) 641-4480

Offers close to four million photos spanning all types of subject matter, including vintage images. Also stocks illustrations.

MIDWEST (IA, IL, IN, MI, MN, MO, OH, WI)

CUSTOM MEDICAL STOCK PHOTO
3821 N. Southport Ave.
Chicago, IL 60613
(800) 373-2677, (312) 248-3200
Fax: (312) 248-7427

Stocks millions of photos and illustrations dealing with scientific subject matter, especially medicine, psychology and chemistry. Offers an electronic bulletin board where images can be previewed on-line. Also will supply images on CD-ROM.

FIRST IMAGE WEST
921 W. Van Buren, Ste. 201
Chicago, IL 60607
(312) 733-9875, (312) 733-2844

Specializes in midwestern and southwestern photography, primarily scenic. Also offers general stock images. Offers preview images on-line as part of PNI (Picture Network International).

MGA/PHOTRI
40 E. 9th St., Ste. 1109
Chicago, IL 60605
(312) 987-0078
Fax: (312) 987-0134

General stock agency offering close to one million contemporary images.

NAWROCKI STOCK PHOTOS
20-L W. 15th St.
Chicago, IL 60605
(800) 356-3066, (312) 427-8625
Fax: (312) 427-0178

Historical photos and etchings, movie stills and a broad range of contemporary subject matter. Known mostly for model release and travel photography. Offers several catalogs specific to certain subject areas.

PANORAMIC STOCK IMAGES
230 N. Michigan Ave.
Chicago, IL 60601
(800) 543-5250, (312) 236-8545
Fax: (312) 704-4077

Offers panoramic landscapes from all over the world—primarily color, contemporary imagery. Specializes in large-format transparencies.

TIP

More and more individuals and stock photo agencies are now offering their services on-line. Check out the Kodak Picture Exchange (an on-line service representing mainly stock photo houses), Picture Network International and the Wieck Photo Database.

THIRD COAST STOCK SOURCE

P.O. Box 92397

Milwaukee, WI 53202

Or:

205 W. Highland Ave., Ste. 507

Milwaukee, WI 53203

(800) 323-9337, (414) 765-9442

Fax: (414) 765-9342

Offers over 300,000 images, mostly general subject matter, as well as regional. Charges no research fee.

TONY STONE IMAGES

500 N. Michigan Ave., Ste. 1700

Chicago, IL 60611

(800) 234-7880, (312) 644-7880

Fax: (312) 644-8851

Contemporary subject matter, mostly lifestyle and travel. Based in London, agency also has offices in New York, Toronto and Los Angeles.

SOUTHWEST (AR, AZ, LA, NM, OK, TX)

ADSTOCK PHOTOS

2614 E. Cheryl Dr.

Phoenix, AZ 85028-4349

(800) 266-5903, (602) 277-5903

Fax: (602) 992-8322

General and regional contemporary subject matter (majority of photogaphers are based west of the Mississippi).

WEATHERSTOCK

P.O. Box 31808

Tucson, AZ 85751

(520) 751-9964, (520) 751-1185

Weather-related imagery. Over ten thousand images of tornadoes, rain, etc. Also has scenic shots. Over ten thousand contemporary images.

WEST (CA, CO, KS, HI, NB, ND, NV, SD, UT, WY)

ALL SPORT PHOTOGRAPHY USA, INC.

320 Wilshire Blvd., Ste. 300

Santa Monica, CA 90401

(310) 395-2955

Fax: (310) 394-6099

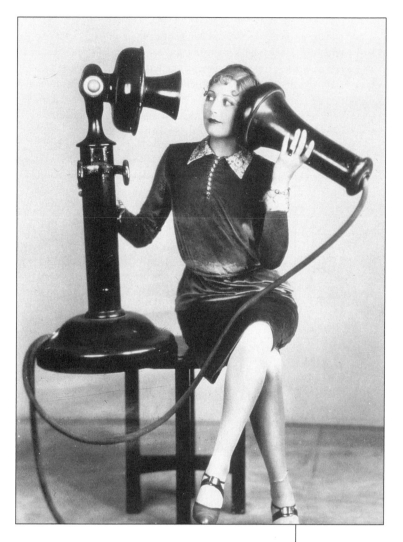

Vintage and contemporary images depicting all kinds of sports. Offers seven million images.

LONG PHOTOGRAPHY

5765 Rickenbacker Rd.

Los Angeles, CA 90040

(213) 888-9944

Fax: (213) 888-9997

Specializes in contemporary sports-related images dating back to the 1970s. Will preview images online and supply customers with images on CD-ROM as well as traditional mediums.

MOUNTAIN STOCK PHOTOGRAPHY AND FILM, INC.

Box 1910

Tahoe City, CA 96145

(916) 583-6646

Fax: (916) 583-5935

Specializes in action lifestyle photographs of hunting, climbing, fishing and other outdoor activities. Also offers shots of mountain scenery.

Superstock offers close to four million photos spanning all types of subject matter, including vintage images such as this one. For further information, see the agency's listing on page 34.

When looking for photos of regional landmarks and geography, don't overlook a city's chamber of commerce as a photo source. The chamber of commerce in a particular locale will generally loan out slides and transparencies for a nominal fee or at no charge—particularly if you're involved in promoting an event which will take place in their area. State and local boards of tourism are also good sources for low-cost visuals, as are universities, government agencies and trade associations.

PACIFIC STOCK
758 Kapahulu Ave., Ste. 250
Honolulu, HI 96816
(800) 321-3239, (808) 735-5665
Fax: (808) 735-7801

Offers a broad range of subjects but specializes in Hawaiian, South Pacific and Asian imagery, including scenic, nature and lifestyle photos from these regions.

PHOTOBANK
17952 Skypark Circle, Ste. B.
Irvine, CA 92714
(800) 383-4084, (714) 250-4480
Fax: (714) 752-5495

Photography, some illustration. Broad subject matter offering about a half million images.

THE PHOTOFILE
48 Century Ln.
Petaluma, CA 94952
(800) 334-5222, (415) 397-3040
Fax: (707) 766-8811

General stock agency offering about one million images, the majority in color. Also offers regional subject matter under the name San Francisco Stock.

SHOOTING STAR INTERNATIONAL PHOTO AGENCY
1441 N. McCaddan Pl.
Hollywood, CA 90028
(213) 469-2020
Fax: (213) 464-0880

Specializes in photos of entertainers, politicians and other celebrities.

STOCK IMAGERY, INC.
711 Kalamuth St.
Denver, CO 80204
(800) 288-3686, (303) 592-2090
Fax: (303) 592-1278

Offers over 100,000 images covering a broad range of subject matter.

STOCKWORKS
11936 W. Jefferson Blvd., Ste. C
Culver City, CA 90230
(310) 390-9744
Fax: (310) 390-3161

Over four hundred images, primarily contemporary.

TERRAPHOTOGRAPHICS/BPS
P.O. Box 490
Moss Beach, CA 94038
(415) 726-6244
Fax: (415) 726-624

Offers close to 100,000 earth, environmental, geological and nature subjects.

TOM STACK AND ASSOCIATES
3645 Jannine Dr., Ste. 212
Colorado Springs, CO 80917
(800) 648-7740, (719) 570-1000
Fax: (719) 570-7290

Agency specializes in international wildlife, nature and space. Over a million images available.

TONY STONE IMAGES
6100 Wilshire Blvd., Ste. 1250
Los Angeles, CA 90048
(800) 234-7880 (213) 938-1700
Fax: (213) 938-0731

Contemporary subject matter, mostly lifestyle and travel. Based in London, agency also has offices in New York, Toronto and Chicago.

WESTLIGHT
2223 S. Carmelina Ave.
Los Angeles, CA 90064
(800) 872-7872, (310) 820-7077
Fax: (310) 820-2687

General subject matter, mostly contemporary. Millions of images available.

ZEPHYR PICTURES
339 N. Highway 101
Solana Beach, CA 92705
(800) 537-3794, (619) 755-1200
Fax: (619) 755-3723

Over 100,000 contemporary images of people and lifestyle subject matter.

NORTHWEST (ID, MT, OR, WA)

ART ON FILE
1837 E. Shelby
Seattle, WA 98112
(206) 322-2638, (206) 329-1928

Offers images of great art and architecture. Special rates available for educational use. Can supply digitized images on CD-ROM as well as traditional photographic formats.

STREANO/HAVENS
P.O. Box 488
Anacortes, WA 98221
(360) 293-4525
Fax: (360) 293-2411

Offers over 150,000 contemporary photos, primarily general subject matter as well as many regional images of the Pacific Northwest.

BUDGET SOURCES FOR STOCK PHOTOGRAPHY

The following government and state-affiliated agencies maintain photo libraries of images that they will rent at a nominal fee or loan for handling charges. Because their research capabilities aren't on a par with commercial agencies, it may take awhile before these agencies can locate what you need. But if you've got the time, they've got the visuals, at prices just about anyone can afford.

HUNT INSTITUTE FOR BOTANICAL DOCUMENTATION
5000 4th Ave., 5th Fl.
Carnegie Mellon University
Pittsburgh, PA 15213
(412) 268-2434
Fax: (412) 268-5677

Specializes in nature scenes and botanical images. Fees start at $4 for a black-and-white print, $20 for a 4"×5" color transparency. Normal turnaround is twenty to thirty working days. Rush service is available for a higher fee.

NASA
400 Maryland Ave. SW, Rm. 6035
Washington, DC 20546
(202) 358-1900

Offers shots of earth from space, space shuttle lift-offs and landings, moon landings, etc. Cost per image ranges from $6 to $10, depending on format.

NATIONAL ARCHIVES AT COLLEGE PARK
8601 Aldelphi Rd.
College Park, MD 20740-6001

The National Archives makes reproductions of its collection available through private vendors. Charges average around $8 for a black-and-white photograph and $10 for a color 35mm slide. Scans are also available on disk and CD-ROM as well as various types of color prints. This agency doesn't respond to phone requests. Write to the address above for a list of vendors and their prices.

NATIONAL PARK SERVICE
Dept. of Public Affairs
1849 C St. NW, Rm. 3424
Washington, DC 20546
ATTN: Rosa Wilson
(202) 208-7394
Fax: (202) 219-0910

Loans color transparencies and black-and-white prints of its parks, monuments and battlegrounds at no charge for most usage situations. Users can keep visuals up to sixty days and, if they wish, can duplicate them during that period.

PHOTOEDITING AND ENHANCING SOFTWARE

These programs can be used to retouch and alter photographic images and otherwise prepare them for print or multimedia.

ADOBE PHOTOSHOP
1585 Charleston Rd.
P.O. Box 7900
Mountainview, CA 94039-7900
(800) 833-6687
(800) 235-0078 (for product literature)

GALLERY EFFECTS
Adobe Systems
411 1st Ave., S.
Seattle, WA 98104-2871
(206) 622-5500
Fax: (206) 343-3360

TIP

Can't find what you need from a stock agency? Need to hire a photographer to get that specific shot? Check the photography organizations in chapter thirteen under Graphic Arts Organizations. They can help direct you to member photographers in your area.

TYPE

Chapter

4

TYPOGRAPHICAL

AIDS AND

SERVICES,

RARE TYPEFACES

AND

COMPUTER FONTS

TYPEHOUSES OFFERING RARE AND UNUSUAL FONTS

In addition to vintage and exotic fonts, the following typehouses offer practically every other imaginable typeface as well as standard faces. Most will take out-of-town orders by fax or modem, but the turnaround times shown may not include overnight shipping.

ALDUS TYPE STUDIO
731 S. LeBrea
Los Angeles, CA 90036
(213) 933-7371
Fax: (213) 933-8613

More than eight thousand headline fonts and two thousand text fonts. Normal turnaround time is twelve to fourteen hours.

ANDRESEN TYPOGRAPHICS (LOS ANGELES)
920 Colorado Ave.
Santa Monica, CA 90401
(310) 452-5521
Fax: (310) 576-1017

About seven thousand headline fonts and four thousand text fonts. Overnight service, with rush service available.

ANDRESEN TYPOGRAPHICS (SAN FRANCISCO)
1500 Sansome St., Ste. 100
San Francisco, CA 94111
(415) 421-2900
Fax: (415) 421-5842

About seven thousand headline fonts and four thousand text fonts. Overnight service, with rush service available.

LATENT SYMPHONY
54 W. 21st St.
New York, NY 10010
(212) 604-0055
Fax: (212) 645-3276

Approximately seven thousand headline fonts and twenty-five hundred text typefaces. Turnaround time is twelve to fourteen hours, with two-hour rush available.

LETTERGRAPHICS INTERNATIONAL
8540 W. Washington Blvd.
Culver City, CA 90230
(213) 870-4828
Fax: (213) 202-0990

More than seven thousand typefaces. Normal turnaround time is twenty-four hours or overnight.

LINOGRAPHIC SERVICES
610 S. Jennings
Fort Worth, TX 76104
(817) 332-4070
Fax: (817) 429-9780

Approximately ten thousand typefaces including some that are hot metal. Turnaround time depends on the client's request.

M&H TYPE
460 Bryant St.
San Francisco, CA 94107
(415) 777-0716
Fax: (415) 777-2730

Offers hot-metal type with about five hundred faces available, many of them vintage. Turnaround time is 24 hours.

OMNICOMP
99 Green St.
San Francisco, CA 94111
(415) 398-3377
Fax: (415) 781-4010

Approximately seven thousand typefaces, half of them exclusively display. Turnaround time is twenty-four hours or overnight.

PACIFIC DIGITAL
1050 Sansome St., Ste. 100
San Francisco, CA 94111
(415) 781-8973
Fax: (415) 781-7465

About ten thousand typefaces, half of them specialty fonts. Turnaround time is normally twenty-four hours or overnight.

PHIL'S PHOTO, INC.
% Dodge Colors' Image Center
7649 Old Georgetown Rd.
Bethesda, MD 20814
(800) 424-2977, (301) 656-0025
Fax: (301) 654-0061

Specializes exclusively in headline fonts, approximately sixty-five hundred of them. Normal turnaround time is overnight or twenty-four hours.

COMPUTER FONTS

The following companies make Macintosh- and PC-compatible computer fonts available on floppy disk, CD-

ROM and in some cases on-line (on an as-needed basis). All of them take phone orders and most will furnish a catalog of their fonts. Those that also sell their fonts through retail outlets are noted.

ADOBE SYSTEMS, INC.

1585 Charleston Rd.
P.O. Box 7900
Mountain View, CA 94039-7900
(800) 833-6687, (415) 961-4400

Over two thousand fonts ranging in price from $49 to $275. Offerings include a collection of fancy capital letters that simulate the look of illustrated book plates as well as Multiple Master typefaces that can be scaled and weighted without destroying integrity of design. Available on diskette and CD-ROM in Mac- and PC-compatible formats.

AGFA TYPE

90 Industrial Way
Wilmington, MA 01887
(800) 424-TYPE, (508) 658-5600
Fax: (508) 657-5328

Over three thousand fonts ranging in price from $25 to $50. Sold in individual volumes from three collections: the Logo and Symbol Collection, the Typographer's Edition (headline and decorative typefaces) and Designer Showcase, 102 cutting-edge typefaces from designers that include T-26, Mark Harris and the Font Bureau. Available on diskette and CD-ROM in Mac- and PC-compatible formats.

ALPHABETS, INC.

P.O. Box 5448
Evanston, IL 60204
(800) 326-4083, (708) 328-2733
Fax: (708) 328-1922

Offers about fifty fonts ranging in price from $109 to $124. Offers typefaces on Design Online to those who are technologically savvy enough to download these fonts via modem on a subscription basis. Collection includes Multiple-Master fonts. Also available on diskette, fonts are Mac- and PC-compatible.

AUTOLOGIC, INC.

1050 Rancho Conejo Blvd.
Thousand Oaks, CA 91320
(800) 457-8973, (805) 498-9611
Fax: (805) 499-1167

Offers about 150 fonts ranging from $23 to $40. Typefaces and borders are especially suited for newspapers, and users include *USA Today*, the *Los Angeles Times* and the *New York Times*. Company also sells Bitstream and Adobe libraries.

International Type Founders is an organization of small type foundries that have joined forces to market their fonts on CD-ROM. Each foundry sets its own prices on a locked CD-ROM that also includes twenty free typefaces and a 240-page specimen book. Cost of the CD-ROM library is $75. Contact ITF at (610) 584-1011.

Available on diskette and CD-ROM in Mac- and PC-compatible formats.

BITSTREAM, INC.

215 First St.
Cambridge, MA 02142
(800) 522-3668, (617) 497-6222

Over one thousand fonts from sources that range from ITC to European foundries. Typefaces include designs commissioned from Herman Zapf and John Downer and traditional favorites. Available on diskette and CD-ROM in Mac- and PC-compatible formats.

CARTER AND CONE TYPE, INC.

2155 Massachusetts Ave.
Cambridge, MA 02140
(800) 952-2129, (617) 576-0398

Offers four fonts designed by Matthew Carter: Big Caslon, Mantinia, Sophia and ITC Galliard. Distributed through Font Haus, Font Shop and Precision Type. Prices range from $60 to $150. Fonts are both Mac- and PC-compatible and available on diskette.

CASADY & GREENE, INC.

22734 Portola Dr.
Salinas, CA 93908-1119
(800) 359-4920, (408) 484-9218

Offers library of fonts of musical symbols and Cyrillic alphabets. Mac- and PC-compatible fonts are available on diskette and start at $40 per font.

CASTLE SYSTEMS

1306 Lincoln Ave.
San Rafael, CA 94901-2105
(415) 459-6495
Fax: (415) 459-6495

Library of thirty fonts consists primarily of resurrected vintage typefaces, including those of art deco and Cyrillic vintage. Available in both Mac and PC formats on diskette; price is $39 per font.

DENIART SYSTEMS

1074 Adelaide Station
Toronto, Ontario M5C 2K5
Canada
(416) 941-0948

Modula Sans

aAbBcCdDeEfFgGhHiIjJkK
lLmMnNoOpPqQrRsStTuUvV
wWxXyYzZ1234567890
aAbBcCdDeEfFgGhHiIjJkK
lLmMnNoOpPqQrRsStTuUv
VwWxXyYzZ1234567890
aAbBcCdDeEfFgGhHiIjJkKL
LmMnNoOpPqQrRsStTuUvV
wWxXyYzZ1234567890

Graphics was one of the first type foundries to bring original digital type designs into desktop mainstream. Shown here is Modula Sans, by Zuzana Licko, one of many typefaces Emigre offers. For more information, see their listing at right.

This small foundry specializes in Morse code, Braille, chemical symbols, Egyptian hieroglyphics and other symbols for communication. Offers twelve fonts on diskette ranging from $39 to $49 per font. Mac- and PC-compatible.

DENNIS ORTIZ-LOPEZ
267 W. 70th St., #2C
New York, NY 10023
(212) 877-6918
Fax: (212) 769-3783

Known for his typeface designs for *Rolling Stone* and other publications, Ortiz-Lopez offers sixty of his fonts on diskette and via modem. Designs include "layers" fonts, and an unusual collection of ornaments and alphabets with drop shadows. Prices for Mac- and PC-compatible fonts range from $30 to $75 per font.

THE ELECTRIC TYPOGRAPHER
2216 Cliff Dr.
Santa Barbara, CA 93109-1270
(805) 966-7563

Small foundry specializes in calligraphic display faces and decorative initials. Library offers overlapping letters and other embellishments that help retain a hand-lettered look. Offers thirty-six fonts ranging in price from $45 to $75 per font. Mac- and PC-compatible.

EMIGRE GRAPHICS
4475 D St.
Sacramento, CA 95819
(800) 944-9021, (916) 451-4344

One of the first type foundries to bring original digital type designs into desktop mainstream, Emigre offers its own designs (many with a "digital" look) as well as those from hot designers. Prices range from $59 to $95 per font. Library of about fifty fonts is available on-line as well as on diskette and CD-ROM. Mac- and PC-compatible.

FONT BUREAU
175 Newbury St.
Boston, MA 02116
(617) 423-8770
Fax: (617) 423-8771

Founded by type designers David Berlow and Roger Black, offerings include "Rolling Stone," originally designed for the magazine whose name it bears. Library consists of close to 250 fonts. Foundry also does custom typefaces. In addition to *Rolling Stone*, clients include *Esquire* and *PC Week*. Available via modem and on diskette, cost is $40 per font. Mac- and PC-compatible.

FONTHAUS, INC.
15 Perry Ave., Ste. A7
Norwalk, CT 06850
(800) 942-9110, (203) 367-1993
Fax: (203) 367-1860

Offering over ten thousand fonts, this clearinghouse represents over sixty independent type designers and foundries. Library includes typefaces from Bitstream, Adobe, Monotype and Autologic. Offers custom packages of client-specified typefaces on diskette. Available in Mac and PC formats on diskette and CD-ROM.

FONTSHOP USA, INC.
47 W. Polk, #100-310
Chicago, IL 60605
(800) 363-6687, (312) 360-1990
Fax: (312) 360-1997

Representing more than thirty independent foundries, this distributor offers font designs from such eminent typographers as Erik Spikerman and Neville Brody. Company also is exclusive dealer of Neville Brody's multimedia publication, *Fuse*. The firm also provides custom design work. Library consists of over four hundred Mac- and PC-compatible fonts at $129 each, available on diskette and CD-ROM.

FOSTER AND HORTON
211 W. Gutirez
Santa Barbara, CA 93101
(805) 962-3964

Offers twenty-four historical display fonts scanned from letterpress originals. Fonts range from $35 to $50 each and are available on diskette. Mac- and PC-compatible.

GARAGEFONTS
703 Stratford Ct., #4
Delmar, CA 92014
(619) 755-4761
Fax: (619) 755-4761

This small foundry offers fonts from *Ray Gun* magazine as well as work from other type designers. Fonts are not intended for text, but are especially well suited to *Ray Gun*-style typographic illustration. Offers over twenty Mac- and PC-compatible fonts on diskette. Prices range from $65 to $100 per font.

HANDCRAFTED FONTS
P.O. Box 14013
Philadelphia, PA 19122
(215) 634-0634

This collection consists of over thirty historically inspired fonts based on samples from late 19th century design movements. Typefaces include rare faces from Art Nouveau, Art Deco and Arts and Crafts movements and include ligatures and ornaments. Firm also offers custom type design. Fonts are Mac- and PC-compatible and are available on diskette and via modem for $35 each.

HOUSE INDUSTRIES
814 N. Harrison St., 36th Fl.
Wilmington, DE 19806
(800) 888-4390, (302) 888-1218
Fax: (302) 888-1650

Offers over twenty-four original typefaces with a contemporary look—some fonts have even turned up in such places as MTV. Offers Mac- and PC-compatible fonts on diskette starting at $40 per font.

IMAGE CLUB GRAPHICS
729 24th Ave., SE
Calgary, Alberta T2G 5K8
Canada
(800) 661-9410, (403) 262-8008
Fax: (403) 261-7013

Over three hundred fonts available in discounted Font-Paks of six to twenty different families, or individually at a cost of $15 to $150 per font. Includes display and picture fonts, as well as text fonts.

Fonts are Mac- and PC-compatible and are available on diskette or CD-ROM. Call for free catalog.

INTERNATIONAL TYPEFACE CORP. (ITC)
866 2nd Ave.
New York, NY 10017
(800) 425-3882, (212) 371-0699
Fax: (212) 752-4752

Formerly sold through other distributors, ITC now retails its extensive line of fonts through ITC Design Palette (see the top of page 8) starting at $60 per font. ITC is continually adding more typefaces to its font collection and publicizes its additions through *U&lc* magazine, its quarterly tabloid (see chapter thirteen under Magazines/Newsletters). Fonts are Mac-compatible and are available on CD-ROM and diskette.

JERRY'S WORLD/THE FONTBANK, INC.
2620 Central St.
Evanston, IL 60201
(708) 328-7380

Offering over two thousand fonts, this library of display and text typefaces is the largest collection available via modem. Potential customers can browse typefaces from CompuServe, download selected fonts, and be billed through their CompuServe account. Fonts are Mac- and PC-compatible and range from $3 to $19.95 each. Also available on CD-ROM.

KAPPA TYPE, INC.
P.O. Box 1652
Palo Alto, CA 94302
(800) 480-0135, (415) 322-0135
Fax: (415) 326-8844

Offers popular typefaces reconfigured for Eastern European languages. Collection of over thirty-five fonts also includes Welsh, Vietnamese and Maltese. PC-compatible fonts range from $70 to $120 and are available on diskette.

House Industries offers some unusual fonts that play on the foundry's "house" theme. Shown is a sampling from the more than thirty fonts House Industry offers. At top is Slawterhouse, designed by Allen Mercer; below is Rougfhouse, by designer Andy Cruz. For more information, see House Industries' listing at left.

KEYSTROKES
Rte. 1, Box 168
Barton, VT 05822
(802) 525-8837

Small foundry specializes in art deco fonts. Library consists of twenty-four display typefaces for $55 each. Mac- and PC-compatible collection is available on diskette.

LANSTON TYPE CO. LTD.
P.O. Box 60
6 Egan St.
Mt. Stewart, PEI C0A 1T0
Canada
(800) 478-8973, (902) 676-2835
Fax: (902) 676-2393

Offers over forty-five fonts that are faithful replicas of the foundry's century-old library of metal fonts. Collection is Mac- and PC-compatible and available on diskette starting at $75 per font. Company also does custom work, including digital logotypes.

LETRASET FONTEK FONTS
40 Eisenhower Dr.
Paramus, NJ 07653
(800) 343-8973, (201) 845-6100

Collection of over 240 fonts includes display and text faces as well as ornaments. Letraset also sells picture fonts (see page 21 in chapter two) and offers a catalog of its fonts, *Font Specifier*, for $16.95. Mac- and PC-compatible fonts are available on CD-ROM and diskette off-the-counter at art and graphics supply stores starting at $39.95.

LETTERPERFECT
6606 Soundview Dr.
Gig Harbor, WA 98335
(800) 929-1951, (206) 851-5158

Collection of over thirty fonts is based on original hand-lettered designs of former greeting card letterer. Mac- and PC-compatible fonts are available on diskette for $39 each.

LINOTYPE-HELL CO.
425 Oser Ave.
Hauppauge, NY 11788
(800) 633-1900, (516) 434-2000

This well-established foundry offers an extensive library of two thousand typefaces accumulated over one hundred-plus years in the business. In addition to fonts that are Mac- and PC-compatible, Linotype-Hell also offers UNIX format and GX-compatible typefaces. Fonts range from $20 to $25 each and are available on diskette and CD-ROM.

MONOTYPE TYPOGRAPHY, INC.
150 S. Wacker Dr., Ste. 2630
Chicago, IL 60606
(800) 666-6897, (312) 855-1440
Fax: (312) 855-9475

Offers Adobe, Monotype and Type Designers of the World fonts. Mac- and PC-compatible fonts are available on diskette and CD-ROM starting at $22.50 per font.

NIMX FOUNDRY
3878 Oaklawn Ave., Ste. 100B-177
Dallas, TX 75219
(800) 688-6469, (214) 350-7930

Offers a small collection of funky display fonts and dingbats. Firm also makes Multiple Master typefaces and a picture font called Faces, which is composed of mix-and-match facial parts.

OLDUVAI CORP.
9200 S. Dadeland Blvd., Ste. 525
Miami, FL 33156
(800) 548-5151, (305) 670-1112

Offers over forty-three fonts in budget packages that contain ten to twenty typefaces apiece. All typefaces include foreign language characters. Mac- and PC-compatible fonts are available on diskette and via modem. Packages range from $129 to $149.

PHIL'S FONTS INC.
℅ Dodge Colors' Image Center
7649 Old Georgetown Rd.
Bethesda, MD 20814
(800) 424-2977, (202) 328-4141
Fax: (202) 328-4138

Collections of fonts from independent designers. Includes Emigre designers, Dennis Ortiz-Lopez, Metal Studio and more.

PRECISION TYPE
47 Mall Dr.
Commack, NY 11725-5703
(800) 248-3668, (516) 864-0167
Fax: (516) 543-5721

Distributes fonts for major and designer foundries as well as font software. Fonts are available on CD-ROM and diskette and include picture fonts as well as text and display typefaces. The company offers a catalog of 571 fonts for $6.95.

PREPRESS SOLUTIONS
11 Mt. Pleasant Ave.
E. Hanover, NJ 07936
(800) 631-8134, (716) 637-9390

This catalog company offers typefaces formerly owned by Varityper. Library also includes fonts from Adobe, Bitstream and other foundries. In addition to text and display fonts, collection includes foreign language fonts. Mac- and PC-compatible fonts start at $39 and are available on diskette.

RED ROOSTER TYPEFOUNDERS
1915 White Hall Rd.
Norristown, PA 19403
(610) 584-1011

Offers over four hundred text and display fonts at a cost of $47 each. Company is constantly adding to its library of typefaces, which includes turn-of-the-century revivals as well as traditional faces. Company also does custom work. Mac- and PC-compatible fonts are available on diskette and CD-ROM.

RUSSIAN TYPE FOUNDRY
490 Chiquita Ave., Ste. 14
Mountain View, CA 94041
(415) 903-9229
Fax: (415) 964-5280

Offers a collection of over seventeen Cyrillic typefaces on diskette. Offers more than sixty fonts total. Mac- and PC-compatible.

STONE TYPE FOUNDRY INC.
626 Middlefield Rd.
Palo Alto, CA 94301
(800) 557-8663, (415) 324-1870
Fax: (415) 324-1783

Founded by reknowned type designer and former Adobe luminary Sumner Stone, this foundry offers some of the most versatile text and display typefaces to be found. Fonts include a text typeface originally designed for *Print* as well as other fonts suitable for magazines and other text-intensive publications. Stone also does custom work. Starting at $59 each, over twenty-four fonts are available on diskette in Mac and PC formats.

T-26
361 W. Chestnut
Chicago, IL 60601
(312) 670-8973

Offers cutting-edge display typefaces designed by founders Carlos Segura and Scott Smith, as well as unusual submissions from other designers from the Chicago area—including Greg Samata, Stephen Farrell and Maoli Marur. Fonts have been seen in a number of places including promotions for *HOW* magazine's annual conference. Starting at $54, over 150 Mac- and PC-compatible fonts are available on diskette and via modem.

THIRSTYPE
117 S. Cook St., Ste. 333
Barrington, IL 60010
(708) 842-0333
Fax: (708) 842-0220

Designer Rick Valicenti, founder of Chicago-based Thirst, offers his own unique fonts, seen in his design concepts for many of Gilbert's paper promotions as well as *Harper's Bazaar*. Collection of six Mac- and PC-compatible fonts is available on diskette starting at $150 each.

TREACYFACES, INC.
111 Sibley Ave.
Ardmore, PA 19003
(203) 389-7037

Thirstype offers original fonts created by its founder, designer Rick Valicenti. Shown are a number of their display faces. See the Thirstype listing at left for more information.

Typefaces designed by Joe Treacy are primarily new text typefaces that are updated versions of traditional looks. Fonts have a reputation for being well-kerned and well-designed. Treacy also does custom work. Catalog is available for $5. Prices start at $14.95 for over two hundred Mac- and PC-compatible fonts available on diskette, CD-ROM and via modem.

URW AMERICA, INC.
4 Manchester St.
Nashua, NH 03060
(800) 229-8791, (603) 882-7445
Fax: (603) 882-7210

Offers over three thousand text and display fonts as well as custom work. Mac- and PC-compatible fonts cost $45 each and are available on CD-ROM and diskette.

Y AND Y
45 Walden St., Ste. 2F
Concord, MA 01742
(800) 742-4059, (508) 371-3286
Fax: (508) 371-2004

Offers over 150 text and mathematical fonts for use in textbooks and diagrams and other technical drawings. Mac- and PC-compatible fonts start at $45 each and are available on diskette.

FONT SOFTWARE

These companies manufacture software that can be used to create computer fonts, enhance the performance of existing fonts, and manipulate fonts to your specifications. Compatibility with Mac and PC equipment is indicated within each software listing.

ADOBE SYSTEMS, INC.
1585 Charleston Rd.
P.O. Box 7900
Mountain View, CA 94039-7900
(800) 833-6687, (415) 961-4400

Offers the following applications:
TypeAlign (Mac)—Creates special typographic effects such as setting type on a curve or creating perspective effects.
TypeManager (Mac)—Provides sharp, smooth type on screen—does away with bitmapped jaggies.
TypeReunion (Mac)—Alphabetizes font menu names and groups styles into sub-menus.
Typestry (Mac, PC)—Creates special effects with type including cutouts, shadows and other 3D effects.

AGFA
90 Industrial Way
Wilmington, MA 01887
(800) 424-TYPE, (508) 658-5600
Fax: (508) 657-5328

Offers the following applications:
KernEdit (Mac)—Creates kerning pairs with page layout and drawing applications.
TypeChart (Mac)—For creating type specimen charts and books.

ARES
565 Pilgrim Dr., Ste. A
Foster City, CA 94404
(415) 578-9090
Fax: (415) 378-8999

Ares FontMinder (PC)—Moves fonts in and out of Windows when needed to avoid keeping them installed all the time.
Ares FontMonger (Mac, PC)—Converts fonts from one format to another.

BITSTREAM, INC.
215 1st St.
Cambridge, MA 02142
(800) 522-3668, (617) 497-6222

MakeUp (PC)—Creates special effects such as stretching, creating drop shadows and embossed type.

BRODERBUND
P.O. Box 6125
Novato, CA 94948-6125
(800) 521-6263
Fax: (415) 382-4419

TypeStyler (Mac)—Allows for blending, stretching, creating drop shadows and creating other special effects.

FIFTH GENERATION/SYMANTEC CORP.
10201 Torre Ave.
Cupertino, CA 95014-2132
(408) 253-9600

Suitcase (Mac)—Eliminates the need to place fonts in your system folder and aids in the organization and identification of fonts.

LETRASET USA
40 Eisenhower Dr.
Paramus, NJ 07653
(800) 526-9073
Fax: (201) 845-5047

Letraset FontStudio (Mac)—Comprehensive font creation and production program.

TIP

A number of the foundries in this chapter offer fonts on-line. If you want to take advantage of this capability, *HOW* magazine's February, 1995, issue offers an excellent article on the topic. "Electric Delivery of Fonts" tells how to get on-line and offers an overview of services.

Letraset LetraStudio (Mac)—Font customization program.

LINOTYPE-HELL CO.
425 Oser Ave.
Hauppauge, NY 11788
(800) 633-1900, (516) 434-2000

Accordion (Mac)—Reduces the number of font menu items displayed by organizing font style variations of a typeface family under the style menu.

Downloader (Mac)—Facilitates speedy installation of printer fonts while saving on disk space.

KeyInfo (Mac)—Creates keyboard layout charts for individual fonts.

SpeedMenu (Mac)—Speeds up font selection by allowing user to scroll through extensive lists of fonts in fractions of a second.

Suitcase Builder (Mac)—Provides flexibility in font organization and management and allows for creating custom screen font suitcases.

MACROMEDIA/ALTSYS
600 Townsend, Ste. 310W
San Francisco, CA 94103
(800) 989-3765, (800) 288-4797, (415) 252-2000

Altsys Fontographer (Mac, PC)—Specialized graphics program that creates and produces fonts.

Altsys Metamorphosis (Mac)—Conversion utility that creates editable outlines and other formats from PostScript and TrueType fonts.

MONOTYPE TYPOGRAPHY, INC.
150 S. Wacker Dr., Ste. 2630
Chicago, IL 60606
(800) 666-6897, (312) 855-1440
Fax: (312) 855-9475

Agency Fit (Mac)—Kerns Macintosh fonts. Comes in two volumes. Combination of two volumes contains kerning pair data for 315 common fonts.

PYRUS NA, LTD.
P.O. Box 465
Millersville, MD 21108
(800) 435-1960, (410) 987-5616
Fax: (410) 987-4980

FontLab (PC)—Creates typefaces, edits typefaces.

TYPE SOLUTIONS
P.O. Box 1227
Plaistow, NH 03865-1227
(603) 382-6400

Incubator Pro (Mac)—Modifies TrueType and PostScript Type 1 fonts so they can be saved in either format.

Incubator for PC (PC)—Modifies any TrueType font by controlling weight, contrast, width and slant.

URW SOFTWARE & TYPE
4 Manchester St.
Nashua, NH 03060
(800) 229-8791, (603) 882-7445
Fax: (603) 882-7210

EuroWorks CD (Mac, PC)—Aids multilingual typesetting.

Ikarus M (Mac)—Program for font, letterform and logotype production.

Kernus (Mac or PC)—Letterspacing tool.

Linus-M (Mac)—Auto-tracing program for incredible accuracy in reproducing alphabets and logotypes.

PAGE LAYOUT SOFTWARE

The following companies manufacture page layout software, useful for creating multi-page documents.

ADOBE PAGEMAKER
411 1st Ave., S.
Seattle, WA 98104-2871
(206) 622-5500
Fax: (206) 343-4240

COREL VENTURA
1600 Carling Ave.
Ottawa, Ontario K1Z 8R7
Canada
(800) 772-6735, (613) 728-3733
Fax: (613) 761-9176

QUARKXPRESS
Quark, Inc.
1800 Grant St.
Denver, CO 80203
(303) 894-8888

CLIP ART ALPHABET SOURCES

THE ART DIRECTOR'S LIBRARY
10 E. 39th St.
New York, NY 10016
(212) 889-6500
Fax: (212) 889-5504

Offers several books of alphabets in calligraphic type, various scripts and Roman styles.

CLIPPER
Dynamic Graphics
6000 N. Forest Park Dr.
P.O. Box 1901
Peoria, IL 61656-9941
(800) 255-8800, (309) 688-8800
Fax: (309) 688-5873

Offers clip alphabets as well as digital files of alphabets.

DOVER PUBLICATIONS, INC.
31 E. 2nd St.
Mineola, NY 11501
(516) 294-7000

Dover publishes many books of copyright-free typography by Dan X. Solo. Each volume is classified by style and contains one hundred complete fonts. Available styles are as follows: Art Deco, Art Nouveau, Bold Script, Circus Alphabets, Condensed Alphabets, Decorative and Display, Gothic and Old English, Outline, Rustic and Rough-Hewn, Sans Serif, Special-Effects and Topical, Stencil, 3-D and Shaded, and Victorian.

MANUFACTURERS OF DRY TRANSFER LETTERING

The products in this listing can be purchased off-the-shelf at art and graphics supply stores. Call manufacturers for a retail outlet in your area.

CHARTPAK
1 River Rd.
Leeds, MA 01053
(800) 628-1910

In addition to dry transfer lettering, company also makes large, self-adhesive letters suitable for display purposes in a variety of colors.

GRAPHIC PRODUCTS CORP.
1480 S. Wolf Rd.
Wheeling, IL 60090-6514
(708) 537-9300

Offers graphic symbols, rules, boxes and borders as well as a variety of headline typefaces. Also sells color, tint and texture films.

LETRASET USA
40 Eisenhower Dr.
Paramus, NJ 07653
(800) 526-9073
Fax: (201) 845-5047

Offers a wide range of rub-down display typefaces, including faces licensed by ITC. Also offers rub-down borders, symbols and other graphic elements as well as tint and texture films.

PACKAGING

Chapter

PACKAGING

MATERIALS

AND

RELATED

SERVICES

boxes

bags

PLASTIC, VINYL AND CELLOPHANE BAGS AND ENVELOPES

Suppliers in this section differ in the type of packaging they offer as well as their ability to handle custom orders. Also check each listing carefully to see if printing capabilities are offered.

ACTION BAG CO.
501 N. Edgewood Ave.
Wood Dale, IL 60191
(708) 766-2881
Fax: (708) 766-3508

Ziploc brand and other plastic bags, cotton drawstring bags, shopping bags and more. Sells small quantities of unprinted bags (up to two thousand). Also does hot-stamp printing for orders of one thousand or more.

BAY WEST PLASTICS, INC.
P.O. Box 334A
West Springfield, MA 01090
(413) 731-8881
Fax: (413) 788-6065

Custom fabricators of heat-sealed vinyl pouches, envelopes and bags. Also has on-site screen printing capability.

CRYSTAL-X CORP.
100 Pine St.
Darby, PA 19023
(800) 255-1160, (610) 586-3200
Fax: (610) 586-3832

Custom and stock boxes, totes, holders, folders, trays and bags.

D&E VINYL CORP.
13524 Vintage Place
Chino, CA 91710
(909) 590-0502
Fax: (909) 591-7822

Custom fabrication of vinyl pouches, bags, binders and folders. Also offers screen printing, embossing and foil-stamp finishing.

KLEER-VU CUSTOM PRODUCTS
51 Kleer-Vu Dr.
Brownsville, TN 38012
(800) 677-3686, (901) 772-2500
Fax: (901) 772-4632

Clear vinyl envelopes, ticket holders, etc. Also makes photo sleeves.

NORTHEAST POLY BAG CO.
2 Northeast Blvd.
P.O. Box 1460
Sterling, MA 01564
(800) 331-8420, (508) 422-3371
Fax: (800) 538-1139

Reclosable bags, mailing bags, poly bags, packing list envelopes and more.

PLASTIC BAGMART
554 Haddon Ave.
Collingswood, NJ 08108
(609) 858-0800
Fax: (609) 854-6006

Clear and solid-colored plastic bags, including Ziploc brand bags. Offers hundreds of different sizes and styles. Doesn't handle printing. Minimum orders depend on size and style.

THE PLASTIC BAG OUTLET
190 W. Passaic St.
Rochelle Park, NJ 07662
(201) 909-0011
Fax: (201) 909-0727

Plastic bags with handles, tote handle bags, garment bags and plastic gloves. Minimum order for custom-imprinted products is ten thousand.

PLASTIC MANUFACTURERS, INC.
3510-28 Scotts Ln.
Philadelphia, PA 19129
(215) 438-1082
Fax: (215) 438-5560

Vinyl envelopes and sleeves. Will print, emboss, apply snaps, punch hangholes, add adhesive backing, grommets and more. Available in clear vinyl and colors.

PLASTIC PRODUCTS CO.
P.O. Box 98
Laurel, MD 20725
(800) 882-1022, (301) 953-2222
Fax: (301) 953-9462

Clear vinyl envelopes and sleeves for documents, photos and badges. Also makes zippered portfolios. Stock and custom designs hot stamped and silkscreened to your specifications.

SACKET CO.
7249 Atoll Ave.
North Hollywood, CA 91605
(818) 764-0110
Fax: (818) 764-1305

Plastic and cellophane bags in over three hundred sizes. Can print up to four colors from customer-supplied art. $25 minimum order required on un-printed bags. Minimums on printed bags vary.

THE TRACIES CO., INC.
100 Cabot St.
Holyoke, MA 01040
(800) 441-7141, (413) 533-7141
Fax: (413) 536-0223

Clear vinyl envelopes for a variety of needs in-cluding bank passbooks, shop envelopes and more. Can customize with hot stamping and screen printing.

CARDBOARD AND PAPER BOXES

A. FLEISIG AND SONS
472 Broadway
New York, NY 10013
(212) 226-7490
Fax: (212) 941-7840

Gift and mailing boxes. Also stocks display boxes with clear acetate windows. Sells plain and custom-printed boxes.

ACORN PAPER PRODUCTS
3686 E. Olympic Blvd.
Los Angeles, CA 90023
(213) 268-0507
Fax: (213) 262-8517

Manufactures printed corrugated boxes. Can print up to four colors.

AGI, INC.
6363 Sunset Blvd., #910
Los Angeles, CA 90028
(213) 462-0821

Manufactures folding cartons and shopping bags. Specializes in music and video carton printing.

DESIGNER PAPER PRODUCTS
45 Prospect St.
Yonkers, NY 10701
(800) 831-7791, (914) 968-6060
Fax: (914) 968-6098

Apparel, jewelry and gift boxes in a variety of col-ors and sizes. Will sell blanks or will custom im-print its products from furnished art. Also sells bags. Minimum order for bags is one thousand.

DORAL PACKAGING CO.
315 Auburn Ave.
P.O. Box 98
Bellefountaine, OH 43311
(800) 241-6834, (513) 592-9785
Fax: (513) 592-1174

Sells plain and custom-printed gift and apparel boxes. Also offers paper and plastic bags.

FIDELITY DIRECT
5601 International Pwy.
P.O. Box 155
Minneapolis, MN 55440-0155
(800) 328-3034
Fax: (800) 842-2725

Shipping boxes, mailing tubes and other types of mailers in hundreds of shapes and sizes. Mini-mum order ranges from fifteen to five hundred, depending on item. Does custom printing from furnished art.

FIRST PACKAGING
2 Mid America Plaza, Ste. 800
Oakbrook Terrace, IL 60181
(312) PACK-AGE
Fax: (708) 665-9822

Corrugated boxes, folding cartons and mailers. Also sells Styrofoam™ and other mailing supplies.

PACKAGING UN-LIMITED, INC.
1121 W. Kentucky St.
Louisville, KY 40210
(800) 234-1833, (502) 584-4331

Manufactures all types of cardboard boxes includ-ing corrugated, gift, jewelry, hat and others. Also offers stock and custom-sized video mailers, book folders, mailing tubes and mailing supplies. Sells unprinted boxes or prints up to four colors on its products from customer-supplied art.

PAPER BAGS

AGI, INC.
6363 Sunset Blvd., #910
Los Angeles, CA 90028
(213) 462-0821

Manufactures folding cartons and shopping bags. Handles music and video carton printing.

paper bags preprinted in a variety of patterns, as well as plastic bags. Will sell blanks, hot-stamp or print bags to customer specifications. Minimum order for bags is five hundred.

DORAL PACKAGING CO.
315 Auburn Ave.
P.O. Box 98
Bellefontaine, OH 43311
(800) 241-6834, (513) 592-9785
Fax: (513) 592-1174

Sells plain and custom-printed merchandise and shopping bags. Also offers plastic bags.

INTERNATIONAL QUALITY PACKAGING
1308 E. 29th St.
Signal Hill, CA 90806
(310) 426-4077
Fax: (310) 426-5886

Four-color shopping bags and other types of merchandise and promotional bags.

LOOSE ENDS
P.O. Box 20310
Keizer, OR 97307
(503) 390-7457
Fax: (503) 390-4724

Offers blank kraft bags in small quantities and bags printed with wildlife motifs. Also offers heavily textured handmade and corrugated papers and boxes, raffia, and other nature-inspired products. Offers free catalog.

PACKAGING UN-LIMITED, INC.
1121 W. Kentucky St.
Louisville, KY 40210
(800) 234-1833, (502) 584-4331

Shopping bags (with rope handles) in matte and glossy finishes. Will print up to four colors from customer-supplied art or sell blank bags. Minimum quantity on unprinted bags is 250.

Designer Paper Products offers blank and custom-printed merchandise and shopping bags, as well as smaller preprinted bags—suitable for cards or small gifts—like the one shown here. They also offer apparel, jewelry and gift boxes in a variety of colors and sizes. See their listing at right for more information.

CRYSTAL TISSUE
P.O. Box 340
Middletown, OH 45042
(513) 423-0731
Fax: (513) 423-0516

Offers shopping and merchandise bags preprinted with stock prints and patterns.

DESIGNER PAPER PRODUCTS
45 Prospect St.
Yonkers, NY 10701
(800) 831-7791, (914) 968-6060
Fax: (914) 968-6098

White and natural craft shopping bags, high-gloss bags and groove-finished bags in a variety of colors. Also sells solid-color paper merchandise bags,

RIGID PLASTIC BOXES

ALPACK, INC.
7-D Overhill Rd.
Natick, MA 01760
(508) 653-9131
Fax: (508) 650-3696

Stock and custom boxes available in a variety of shapes and sizes.

ALTHOR PRODUCTS

496-B Danbury Rd.
Wilton, CT 06897
(800) 688-2693, (203) 762-0796
Fax: (203) 762-3180

Clear plastic boxes. Stock items include hinged or non-hinged in square, rectangular and round. Also offers foam inserts, labels, vials and polybags. Small orders accepted.

CLASSIC LINE

5915-T 21st St.
Racine, WI 53406
(800) 394-7658, (414) 544-4412
Fax: (414) 554-8370

Fully transparent, rigid-molded plastic boxes in a variety of shapes and sizes. Clear and colored plastic available as well as custom imprinting.

GARY PLASTIC PACKAGING CORP.

770 Garrison Ave.
Bronx, NY 10474
(800) 221-8150, (718) 893-2200
Fax: (718) 378-2141

Offers over 350 stock sizes and shapes in rigid plastic boxes. Also does custom designed plastic packaging and can customize stock boxes.

MTM MOLDED PRODUCTS

3370 Obco Ct.
Dayton, OH 45414
(513) 890-7376
Fax: (513) 890-1747

Custom and stock rigid, plastic boxes. Decorating and foam inserts available. Sizes range from $2'' \times 2'' \times 1.25''$ to $21'' \times 9'' \times 9''$.

TRISTATE PLASTICS

P.O. Box 6
Dixon, KY 42409
(800) 951-1551, (502) 639-9142
Fax: (502) 639-5882

Crystal clear boxes. Square, round and rectangular shapes (with lids) in a range of sizes.

PLASTIC BOTTLES, TUBES, BOXES, JARS AND JUGS

ALL-PAK PLASTIC BOTTLES

2260-T Roswell Dr.
Pittsburgh, PA 15205
(800) 245-2283, (800) 245-2284, (412) 922-7525
Fax: (412) 922-0139

Wide range of stock sizes and shapes as well as custom molds. Also creates barrier bottles. Complete decorating service available.

ALPACK, INC.

7-D Overhill Rd.
Natick, MA 01760
(508) 653-9131
Fax: (508) 650-3696

Stock and custom boxes. Also carries jars, vials, tubes, clamshells and carrying cases.

ALPHA PLASTICS, INC.

10315 Page Industrial Blvd.
St. Louis, MO 63132
(800) 421-4772, (314) 427-4300
Fax: (314) 427-5445

Specializes in FDA compliance for medical, pharmaceutical and food industries. Offers custom and stock bottle designs.

ALTIRA, INC.

3225 NW 112 St.
Miami, FL 33167
(305) 687-8074
Fax: (305) 688-8029

Custom bottle designs including 3-D models and prototypes. Does silkscreening, hot stamping, therimage and pad printing.

BERMAN BROS., INC.

1501-T S. Laflin St.
Chicago, IL 60608-2199
(800) 255-4035, (312) 226-4035
Fax: (312) 226-4850

Factory representative for stock bottles, jars, vials, tubes, dispensers, pouches, sprayers and other closures. Offers design consulting, silkscreening, hot stamping, therimage, pressure-sensitive and applied color labelling and frosting.

Continental Glass & Plastic, Inc., manufactures plastic bottles, jars and tubes as well as glass containers. See the company's listing on this page for more information.

BOTTLEWERKS, INC.
9535-T S. Cottage Grove Ave.
Chicago, IL 60628
(312) 978-5930
Fax: (312) 734-6395

A variety of container types in sizes two ounces to thirty-two ounces. Offers silkscreen, therimage and hot-stamp decorating.

CAPTIVE PLASTICS, INC.
251 Circle Dr., N.
Piscataway, NJ 08854-0277
(800) 966-2558, (908) 469-7900
Fax: (908) 356-9487

Stock and custom-designed containers. Provides caps and closures, flame treating, silkscreening and hot stamping, as well as pressure-sensitive and heat transfer labeling. Regional offices in New Jersey, Iowa and California.

CONTINENTAL GLASS & PLASTIC, INC.
841 W. Cermak Rd.
Chicago, IL 60608
(800) 787-JARS, (312) 666-2050
Fax: (312) 243-3419

Offers a wide variety of bottles, tubes, vials and jars. Also provides closures, caps and sprayers as well as many kinds of decorating options including pressure-sensitive labels. Printing options include flexography, foil-stamping, lacquer varnishes, letterpress and screen printing.

CRAWFORD INDUSTRIES
1414 Crawford Dr.
P.O. Box 191
Crawfordsville, IN 47933
(800) 428-0840, (317) 362-6733
Fax: (800) 962-3343

Stock and custom polyethylene boxes for sales presentations, gift boxes and storage units. Screen printing, foil-stamping and debossing decoration are offered.

CROWN GLASS CORP.
2345-T W. Hubbard St.
Chicago, IL 60612-1490
(800) 621-4620, (312) 666-2000
Fax: (312) 666-1505

Stock plastic bottles, jars and jugs and closures for immediate shipment.

DISPLAY PACK
1340 Monroe, NW
Grand Rapids, MI 49505
(616) 451-3061
Fax: (616) 451-8907

Clear plastic blister packs and clamshells. Point-of-purchase trays. Also will do custom thermoforming.

FLAMBEAU PRODUCTS
P.O. Box 1139
Middlefield, OH 44062
(800) 457-5252
Fax: (216) 632-1581

Clear, plastic boxes with hinged and non-hinged lids. Also offers compartmentalized boxes. Available in stock and custom colors and sizes.

FREUND CAN CO.
167 W. 84th St.
Chicago, IL 60620-1298
(312) 224-4230
Fax: (312) 224-8812

Offers bottles, jars and jugs in a wide variety of styles and sizes. Offers immediate shipment even of very low quantities.

INPAC
1014 E. Algonquin Rd.
Schaumburg, IL 60173
(708) 397-9555
Fax: (708) 397-6888

Custom manufacturer of bottles, jars and other types of containers. Also makes closures and provides silkscreening and labeling. Makes prototypes and models.

LEE CONTAINER CORP.
100 Chambers Blvd.
Clinch Industrial Park
Homerville, GA 31634
(912) 487-3631, (912) 487-3632

Stock containers including one- to two and a half-gallon rectangular and round bottles.

THE LERMAN CONTAINER CORP.
10 Great Hill Rd.
P.O. Box 979
Naugatuck, CT 06770
(203) 723-6681
Fax: (203) 723-6687

Offers custom design and an extensive line of stock containers as well as metal and plastic screw caps, dispensing caps, cups and sprayers. Also does hot stamping, sleeve-labeling, therimage, offset and silkscreen labeling. Specializes in tamper-evident packaging.

MAYFAIR PLASTICS
1500 E. 223rd St.
Carson, CA 90745
(800) 486-5428, (310) 952-8736
Fax: (800) 789-9976, (310) 830-0654

Offers custom and stock designs in plastic containers. Decorating available on pressure-sensitive, sleeve and heat transfer labels.

NATIONAL PACKAGING CORP.
411 N. Reynoldsburg-New Albany Rd.
P.O. Box 13256
Columbus, OH 43213
(800) 206-2857, (614) 864-1700
Fax: (800) 206-2858

Stock containers ranging from two ounces to seven gallons. Also manufactures custom designs and provides screen printing and a wide range of closures. Regional offices in Louisville, Kentucky, and Cincinnati, Ohio.

NORTHWESTERN BOTTLE CO.
460 N. Lindbergh Blvd.
St. Louis, MO 63141
(800) 325-7782, (314) 569-3633
Fax: (314) 569-2772

Consultants for custom package design. Distributors in Atlanta, Boston, Chicago, Indianapolis, Kansas City, Los Angeles, Memphis, New Castle, Omaha, Orlando, Phoenix, St. Louis, San Francisco and Syracuse.

PACKAGE SUPPLY & EQUIPMENT CO., INC.
P.O. Box 19021
Greenville, SC 29602
(803) 277-0900
Fax: (803) 277-0957

Bottles, jars, jugs and pails as well as all types of closures. Stock and custom designs available. Also

screen prints on its products. Distribution centers in Atlanta, Charlotte, Nashville, Richmond, Orlando and Cincinnati.

PAN-AM PLASTICS
3555-T S. Normal Ave.
Chicago, IL 60609
(800) 43-SELAR, (312) 373-4200
Fax: (312) 373-2187

Stock and custom blow-molding containers in barrier-resin and high-density polyethylene plastic. Custom decorating as well as caps and closures also available.

PVC CONTAINER CORP.
400 Industrial Way, W.
P.O. Box 597
Eatontown, NJ 07724
(908) 542-0060
Fax: (908) 542-7706

Stock bottle sizes ranging from one ounce to sixty-four ounces. Offers custom designs up to 128 ounces. In-house decorating options include silkscreening, hot stamping, heat transfer and pressure-sensitive labeling.

RIVER SIDE MANUFACTURING
10390 Bermuda Ct.
Bullhead City, AZ 86440
(800) 232-2631, (602) 768-1771
Fax: (602) 768-1770

Makes tubes, bottles, jars, cans and containers in a broad range of sizes. Also does labeling and screen printing on containers. Features low minimum runs.

ROSBRO PLASTICS CO.
999 Main St.
Pawtucket, RI 02860
(401) 723-8400
Fax: (401) 725-3510

Manufactures custom-molded bottles, jars and jugs. Specializes in bottles from two ounces to sixty-four ounces and wide-mouth jars.

SHO-ME CONTAINER, INC.
704-T Pinder Ave.
Grinnell, IA 50112
(800) 394-7504, (515) 236-4798
Fax: (800) 959-0394

Stock plastic cans and jars with screw caps. Also offers in-house silkscreening.

If you've ever wondered how design firms come up with their studios' own brands of custom-labeled and packaged wines, it's not all that difficult. Albuquerque-based Vaughn Wedeen Creative produced twelve cases of custom-labeled and boxed wine to give its clients as holiday gifts. The firm first contacted a small winery in the Albuquerque area and ordered 144 unlabeled bottles of a particular vintage. Vaughn Wedeen had labels printed separately and affixed them to each of the bottles with spray adhesive (a tedious job made more agreeable by sampling some of the wine). To complete the package, the firm contacted a carton manufacturer specializing in styrofoam fitted boxes used for shipping glassware. Matching custom labels were then affixed to these boxes with spray adhesive.

SMITH CONTAINER
3500 Browns Mill Rd., SE
P.O. Box 82566
Atlanta, GA 30354-0566
(404) 768-8725
Fax: (404) 763-1747

Offers jugs, cans, bottles and jars as well as accompanying closures. District operations in Charlotte, Richmond, Memphis, Tampa, Orlando and Tulsa.

W. BRAUN CO.
300 N. Canal
Chicago, IL 60606
(800) 368-6556, (312) 346-6500

Offers a wide range of containers for cosmetic and over-the-counter household chemical, food and novelty industries. Custom and stock designs and closures.

WHINK
1901 15th Ave., Dept. S1
Eldora, IA 50627
(800) 959-0873, (515) 858-2353
Fax: (515) 858-2485

Specializes in containers that meet FDA standards for food, medical and pharmaceutical industries. Offers screen printing, hot stamping and pressure-sensitive labeling.

GLASS CONTAINERS

ALL CONTAINER CORP./HOUSE OF CANS
7060 N. Lawndale Ave.
Lincolnwood, IL 60645
(708) 677-2100
Fax: (708) 677-2103

Distributes a full line of stock glass bottles in sizes ranging from one-half ounce to fifty-five gallons, as well as boxes, jars, cans, jugs, closures and more. Can handle quantities from one to a truckload.

ALLOMETRICS, INC.
11386 Darryl Dr.
P.O. Box 15825
Baton Rouge, LA 70815
(504) 272-4484
Fax: (504) 272-0844

Bottles, jugs, vials and closures. Can fill small orders.

ALL-PAK
2260-T Roswell Dr.
Pittsburgh, PA 15205
(800) 245-2283, (800) 245-2284, (412) 922-7525
Fax: (412) 922-0139

Offers a wide range of stock sizes and shapes as well as custom molds. Also creates barrier bottles. Complete decorating service available.

BERMAN BROS., INC.
1501-T S. Laflin St.
Chicago, IL 60608-2199
(800) 255-4035, (312) 226-4035
Fax: (312) 226-4850

Factory representative for stock bottles, jars, vials, tubes, dispensers, pouches, sprayers and other closures. Offers design consulting, silkscreening, hot stamping, therimage, pressure-sensitive and applied color labeling and frosting.

CHAMPION CONTAINER
180 Essex Ave.
Aveno, NJ 07001
(908) 636-6700
Fax: (908) 855-8663

Bottles and wide-mouth jars in flint and amber.

CONTINENTAL GLASS & PLASTICS, INC.
817 W. Cermak Rd.
Chicago, IL 60608
(800) 787-JARS, (312) 666-2050
Fax: (312) 243-3419

Offers a wide variety of bottles, tubes, vials and jars. Also provides closures, caps and sprayers as well as many kinds of decorating options, including pressure-sensitive labels. Printing options include flexography, foil-stamping, lacquer varnishes, letterpress and screen printing.

CROWN GLASS CORP.
2345-T W. Hubbard St.
Chicago, IL 60612-1490
(800) 621-4620, (312) 666-2000
Fax: (312) 666-1505

Distributor of stock glass bottles, jars and jugs and closures. Products are available for immediate shipment.

INPAC
1014 E. Algonquin Rd.
Schaumburg, IL 60173
(708) 397-9555
Fax: (708) 397-6888

Custom manufacturer of bottles, jars and other types of containers. Also makes closures and provides silkscreening and labeling. Makes prototypes and models.

THE LERMAN CONTAINER CORP.
10 Great Hill Rd.
P.O. Box 979
Naugatuck, CT 06770
(203) 723-6681
Fax: (203) 723-6687

Offers custom design and an extensive line of stock containers as well as metal and plastic screw caps, dispensing caps, cups and sprayers. Also does hot-stamping, sleeve-labeling, therimage, offset and silkscreen labeling. Specializes in tamper-evident packaging.

NATIONAL PACKAGING CORP.
411 N. Reynoldsburg-New Albany Rd.
P.O. Box 13256
Columbus, OH 43213
(800) 206-2857, (614) 864-1700
Fax: (800) 206-2858

Stock containers ranging from two ounces to seven gallons. Also manufactures custom designs and provides screen printing and a wide range of closures. Regional offices in Louisville, Kentucky, and Cincinnati, Ohio.

PACKAGE SUPPLY & EQUIPMENT CO., INC.
P.O. Box 19021
Greenville, SC 29602
(803) 277-0900
Fax: (803) 277-0957

Bottles, jars and jugs as well as all types of closures. Stock and custom designs available. Also does screen printing on its products. Distribution centers in Atlanta, Charlotte, Nashville, Richmond, Orlando and Cincinnati.

ROTH GLASS CO.
171 Steuben St.
Pittsburgh, PA 15220
(412) 921-2095
Fax: (412) 921-8003

Manufactures glass medicine dropper assemblies. Styles, lengths and diameters to client specifications.

SMITH CONTAINER
3500 Browns Mill Rd., SE
P.O. Box 82566
Atlanta, GA 30354-0566
(404) 768-8725
Fax: (404) 763-1747

Offers jugs, cans, bottles and jars as well as accompanying closures, including sprayers and pumps. District operations in Charlotte, Richmond, Memphis, Tampa, Orlando and Tulsa.

Vaughn Wedeen Creative produced twelve cases of custom-labeled and boxed wine to give to their clients as a holiday gift. If you're interested in doing something similar, take a look at the top of page 56 for more details.

COATED GLASSWARE

These companies manufacture glass containers that are treated with shatter- and/or solvent-resistant coatings. Some will also coat customer-furnished glassware.

ALL-PAK
1195 Washington Pike
Bridgeville, PA 15017
(800) 245-2283, (412) 257-3000
Fax: (412) 257-3001

Pre-coated jugs, bottles and jars in amber and flint.

CAROLINA GLASCOAT, INC.
116 Ryan Patrick Dr.
Salisbury, NC 28144
(800) 894-2725, (704) 633-2100
Fax: (704) 633-3420

Stock items include jugs and bottles in flint and amber. Also decorates its products. Will coat customer-furnished glassware.

WHEATON COATED PRODUCTS
5176 Harding Hwy.
Mays Landing, NJ 08330-2298
(800) 453-6377, (609) 625-2291
Fax: (609) 625-7173

Carries pre-coated jugs, jars and bottles. Also custom coats glass from other manufacturers.

METAL CONTAINERS

AMERICAN ALUMINUM CO.
230-T Sheffield St.
Mountainside, NJ 07092
(908) 233-3500
Fax: (908) 233-3241

Manufactures seamless aluminum bottles and tamper-proof closures.

NATIONAL PACKAGING CORP.
411 N. Reynoldsburg-New Albany Rd.
P.O. Box 13256
Columbus, OH 43213
(800) 206-2857
Fax: (800) 206-2858

Stock containers ranging from two ounces to seven gallons. Also manufactures custom designs and provides screen printing and a wide range of closures. Regional offices in Louisville, Kentucky, and Cincinnati, Ohio.

PACKAGE SUPPLY & EQUIPMENT CO., INC.
P.O. Box 19021
Greenville, SC 29602
(803) 277-0900
Fax: (803) 277-0957

Bottles, jars, jugs and pails as well as all types of closures. Stock and custom designs available. Also does screen printing on its products. Distribution centers in Atlanta, Charlotte, Nashville, Richmond, Orlando and Cincinnati.

SMITH CONTAINER
3500 Browns Mill Rd., SE
P.O. Box 82566
Atlanta, GA 30354-0566
(404) 768-8725
Fax: (404) 763-1747

Distributes all types of metal containers and accompanying closures. District operations in Charlotte, Richmond, Memphis, Tampa, Orlando and Tulsa.

OTHER

ANDREW M. MARTIN CO., INC.
P.O. Box 6567
Los Angeles, CA 90734-6567
(800) 286-0460, (213) 775-6101
Fax: (800) 768-5790

Specializes in pillow packs, polysqueeze tubes and pouch packs. Stock and custom designs. Handles manufacture and decorating.

ASPEN PACKAGING
570-J Rock Rd.
East Dundee, IL 60118
(800) 367-5493, (708) 428-8555
Fax: (708) 428-3540

Video packaging and mailers. Custom-imprinted from supplied art, film and digital files. Offers about fifty different styles and sizes. Order minimum is five hundred.

DESIGN PLASTICS
3550 N. Keystone Dr.
Omaha, NE 68134
(800) 491-0786
Fax: (800) 881-0297

Clear plastic blister packs and clamshells, and packaging for compact discs. Also manufactures custom designs in plastic.

FLURO-SEAL, INC.
15915 Katy Frwy., Ste. 205
Houston, TX 77094
(713) 578-1440
Fax: (713) 578-3159

Company provides a post-manufacture finishing process that protects plastic against chemical corrosion. Also protects against discoloration, odor emission, and flavor or fragrance loss.

JAMES ALEXANDER CORP.
RD 3, Box 192, Rte. 94
Blairstown, NJ 07825
(908) 362-9266
Fax: (908) 362-5019

Specialists in custom packaging. Will work with designers to come up with packaging strategy that meets client's objectives.

LOOSE ENDS
P.O. Box 20310
Keizer, OR 97307
(503) 390-7457
Fax: (503) 390-4724

Offers wooden boxes with sliding lids. Also offers heavily textured handmade and corrugated papers, tissue paper, raffia and other nature-inspired products. Small quantities are no problem. Offers a free catalog.

PACKAGE WORKS
1995 Broadway, Ste. 4-3
New York, NY 10023
(212) 769-2552
Fax: (212) 769-3225

Works with designers to fashion custom packaging that encompasses a variety of package types, as well as printed packaging that incorporates clever folds and diecuts.

THIBIANT INTERNATIONAL
8601 Wilshire Blvd., Ste. 1100
Beverly Hills, CA 90211
(800) 375-7110, (310) 659-3347
Fax: (310) 659-4714

Specializes in packaging for skin care, hair care and fragrance industries.

PACKAGING PRINTERS

SILKSCREEN PRINTING

These printers will print directly onto objects such as jars and bottles. Also check listings for plastic and glass containers. Many container manufacturers also offer container printing.

ALPHA PLASTICS, INC.
10315 Page Industrial Ct.
St. Louis, MO 63132
(800) 421-4772, (314) 427-4300
Fax: (314) 427-5445

ALTIRA, INC.
3225-T NW 112th St.
Miami, FL 33167
(305) 687-8074
Fax: (305) 688-8029

BERMAN BROS., INC.
1501-T S. Laflin St.
Chicago, IL 60608
(800) 255-4035, (312) 226-4035, (312) 226-4850

BOTTLEWERKS, INC.
9535-T S. Cottage Grove Ave.
Chicago, IL 60628
(312) 978-5930
Fax: (312) 734-6395

EMPAK
950 Lake Dr., Dept. TR
Chanhassen, MN 55317
(800) 341-4576, (612) 474-5282
Fax: (612) 949-1288

IMTRAN INDUSTRIES, INC.
25 Hale St.
Newburyport, MA 01950
(508) 462-2722
Fax: (508) 462-3113

LABELS, DECALS AND WRAPPERS

The following printers offer a variety of printing techniques, including flexography, letterpress and silkscreen, as well as a wide range of label and decal types, shapes and sizes. In addition to label types mentioned, most also produce bar code labels. Don't overlook listings for plastic and glass containers. Many container manufacturers also offer label printing on labels that will fit their containers.

ALL LABEL CORP.
2194 NW 18th Ave.
Miami, FL 33142
(305) 547-2184
Fax: (305) 325-1842

One-color to four-color process printing on acetate, Mylar, paper and foil. Custom die cutting and waterproofing also available.

AMERICAN LABEL
18951 Bonanza Way
Gaithersburg, MD 20879
(800) 438-3568, (301) 670-6170
Fax: (301) 869-2624

Tags, decals and labels. Also prints control panels and name badges. Screen printing on all types of surfaces including acryllics, plastic, vinyl, foil and metal.

ANDREWS DECAL CO., INC.
6559 N. Avondale Ave., Dept. N
Chicago, IL 60631-1521
(312) 775-1000
Fax: (312) 775-1001

Offers decals, nameplates, computer and pressure-sensitive labels. Flexography, letterpress and silk-screening available. Will print on a variety of materials.

BAY AREA LABELS
1980 Lundy Ave.
San Jose, CA 95131
(800) 229-5223, (408) 432-1980
Fax: (408) 434-6407

Decals and labels from Lexan, polyester, paper and other materials. Offers a variety of print applications, embossing, debossing and holograms. Also makes nameplates and touch-sensitive membrane switches.

BAY TECH LABEL, INC.
13161 56th Ct., #204
Clearwater, FL 34620-4027
(800) 229-8321, (813) 223-7128, (813) 572-8345

Prints from one-color to four-color process. Laminating and varnishing also available.

CLASSIC LABELS
130-T New Haven Rd.
Seymour, CT 06483
(203) 881-9855
Fax: (203) 881-9851

Custom printed pressure-sensitive labels on rolls, sheets and pin-fed. Materials for all applications.

CREATIVE LABELS, INC.
13165 Monterey Rd.
San Martin, CA 95046
(408) 683-0633
Fax: (408) 683-0317

Custom multicolor labels for food, software and more. Also does hang-tags, cards and coupons. Offers short runs with no minimums.

CUMMINS LABEL CO.
2230 Glendening Dr.
Kalamazoo, MI 49003-2042
(616) 345-3386
Fax: (616) 345-6657

Stock and custom-printed labels for many applications, including shipping and packaging. Offers letterpress, flexography and silkscreen printing. No minimum on orders placed.

DELPRINT
2010 S. Carboy
Mt. Prospect, IL 60056
(800) 999-5301, (708) 364-6000
Fax: (708) 364-6012

Custom pressure-sensitive labels for packaging and other applications. Also offers in-mold decorating, heat transfers, rub-down products and five types of printing processes.

DESIGN MARK INDUSTRIES
3 Kendrick Rd.
Wareham, MA 02571
(800) 642-7537, (508) 295-9591
Fax: (508) 295-6752

Custom labels, decals and nameplates. Offers one-to four-color process, offset, flexographic and screen printing as well as hot stamping and embossing. District offices in Raleigh, North Carolina, and Philadelphia, Pennsylvania.

FLEXO TRANSPARENT, INC.
28 Wasson St.
P.O. Box 128
Buffalo, NY 14240
(800) 33-FLEXO, (716) 825-7710
Fax: (716) 825-0139

Manufactures bottle sleeve labels. Stock and custom designs available.

GO TAPE AND LABEL, INC.

19575 NE 10 Ave.
Miami, FL 33179
(800) 468-2731, (305) 652-8300
Fax: (305) 652-8306

Custom labels, tags and tape in all sizes and shapes. Offers one- to four-color process, silk-screening and hot stamping.

GRAFSTICK TAPE & LABEL

P.O. Box 3277
Framingham, MA 01701
(800) 537-6483, (508) 620-6228
Fax: (508) 620-6229

Custom and pre-printed labels in stock.

IDENTIFICATION PRODUCTS CORP.

104 Silliman Ave.
P.O. Box 3276
Bridgeport, CT 06605-0276
(800) 243-9888, (203) 334-5969
Fax: (203) 334-5038

Custom labels on Lexan, foil, vinyl, Mylar and paper. Also makes aluminum nameplates.

INTERMEC MEDIA PRODUCTS

9290 LeSaint Dr.
Fairfield, OH 45014-5454
(800) 881-1303, (513) 874-5882
Fax: (513) 874-8487

Bar code labels, tags and ribbons on thermal and thermal transfer papers, plastics and synthetics.

LABELS AND DECALS, INC.

1450-T Pratt Blvd.
Elk Grove Village, IL 60007
(800) 253-3225, (708) 593-3200
Fax: (708) 593-4257

Labels, nameplates and decals of all types and sizes. Printing applications include flexography, letterpress and silkscreening.

NAMEPLATES FOR INDUSTRY, INC.

213A Rice Blvd.
Industrial Park
New Bedford, MA 02745
(800) 999-8900, (508) 998-9021
Fax: (508) 995-0099

Offers labels, nameplates, decals and tags screen printed to client specifications. Call for free catalog and samples.

PRECISION TAPE & LABEL, INC.

P.O. Box 374
Millbury, MA 01527-0374
(800) 225-7754, (508) 865-1157
Fax: (508) 865-1161

Custom designed labels in up to six colors.

REED-RITE RELIABLE LABEL CO.

2201 Curtiss St.
Downers Grove, IL 60515
(800) 323-7265, (708) 852-5300
Fax: (708) 852-9604

Decals, pressure-sensitive and static cling labels. Available on rolls and sheets. Offers hot stamping and foil labels.

SCREENPRINT/DOW

271-T Ballardvale St.
P.O. Box 1332
Wilmington, MA 01887
(617) 935-6395
Fax: (508) 658-2307

Nameplates, roll labels and control panels. Offers offset and screen printing, letterpress, hot stamping and flexography.

SETON INDUSTRIES

P.O. Box DR-1331
New Haven, CT 06505
(800) 243-6624, (203) 488-8059
Fax: (800) 256-2116

Custom and stock labels, decals and nameplates on vinyl, polyester, paper, foil and metallic substrates. Call for free catalog and samples.

SHORT RUN LABELS

1681 Industrial Rd.
San Carlos, CA 94070
(800) 522-5383, (415) 592-7683
Fax: (800) 456-5575

Specializes in small quantities of self-adhesive labels.

TECHPRINT

28 6th Rd.
Woburn, MA 01888
(800) 225-2538, (617) 933-8420
Fax: (617) 933-7399

Manufactures custom labels on rolls, strips and as individual pieces. Offset and screen printing, flexography and hot stamping. Also offers nameplates, decals and other items.

TIP

Most product packaging requires a UPC (Universal Product Code)—the lines read by laser scanners at checkout counters. To find out how to obtain a code, contact the Universal Code Council, 8163 Old Yankee Rd., Ste. J, Dayton, OH 45458; (513) 435-3870.

WESTERN LABEL CO., INC.
5305 Alhambra Ave.
Los Angeles, CA 90032
(213) 225-2284
Fax: (213) 225-0740

Offers a wide range of labels, decals, tags and nameplates. Printing applications include flexography, letterpress, silkscreening, hot stamping and embossing. Offers up to twelve-color printing.

ENVIRONMENTAL GRAPHICS

Chapter **6**

SIGN AND

DISPLAY

MATERIALS

AND

SERVICES

Sign-making Software

SIGN-MAKING SUPPLIES

When making your own signs, these resources will help supply you with what you need. As a rule, sign blanks, banners and other sign-making materials can be purchased locally—check the business to business directory in your area under "signs—equipment and supplies." Note: Firms preceded by an asterisk (*) are members of the Society of Environmental Graphic Designers (SEGD). For more information on this organization, see the listing in chapter thirteen under Graphic Arts Organizations.

ALUMA PANEL, INC.
2410 Oak St. W.
Cumming, GA 30131
(800) 258-3003, (404) 889-3996
Fax: (404) 889-8972

Aluminum, styrene and other types of sign blanks in a variety of sizes. Also offers sign stands, magnetic sheeting, corrugated plastic, blank banners and sandblast stencils.

AMERICRAFT CORP.
904 4th St., W.
Palmetto, FL 34221
(813) 722-6631
Fax: (813) 723-2452

Plastic and Plexiglas™ letters (and dimensional letters from other materials), sign panels, changeable copy and more.

ART ESSENTIALS OF NEW YORK, LTD.
3 Cross St.
Suffern, NY 10901
(800) 283-5323, (914) 368-1100
Fax: (914) 368-1535

Gold leaf in sheets and rolls and related supplies and tools. Also offers silver leaf.

BARCLAY LEAF IMPORTS, INC.
21 Wilson Terrace
Elizabeth, NJ 07208
(908) 353-5522
Fax: (908) 353-5525

Gold leaf and related supplies. Includes introductory packages.

BEST BUY BANNER CO.
6750 Central Ave.
Riverside, CA 92504
(800) 624-1691, (909) 351-0761
Fax: (909) 351-0618

Blank banners in twenty-four different colors, trimmed and hemmed to your specifications. Sold by the foot.

DICK BLICK
P.O. Box 1267
Galesburg, IL 61302
(800) 447-8192, (309) 343-6181
Fax: (309) 343-5785

Arts and crafts supplies as well as graphics and sign-making supplies. Offers airbrushes, banners, sign blanks and sign cloth, gold leaf, and supplies for pinstriping and screen printing. Also sells books on lettering and sign-related topics.

GOLD LEAF & METALLIC POWDERS, INC.
74 Trinity Place, Ste. 1807
New York, NY 10006
(800) 322-0323, (212) 267-4900
Fax: (212) 608-4245

Genuine metallic leaf including gold, silver, palladium, copper, bronze and other composition leaf products. Also offers gilding supplies and restoration aids.

GRAPHIKORE
Baltek Corp.
10 Fairway Ct.
Northvale, NJ 07647
(201) 767-1400

Wooden sign blanks for sandblasting and carving. Also sells through local distributors.

HARTCO INC.
1280 Glendale-Milford Rd.
Cincinnati, OH 45215
(800) 543-1340, (513) 771-4430
Fax: (513) 771-3327

Sandmask stencils for sandblasting wood, plastic or glass, etching tape, pin-feed stencil materials and more.

MULLER STUDIOS SIGN CO.
59 Ridge Rd.
Stafford Springs, CT 06076
(203) 974-2161
Fax: (same)

Wooden sign blanks in a variety of stock sizes and shapes including oval, rectangular, old-tavern and other vintage looks. Also offers custom wooden signs built to specifications.

NUDO PRODUCTS, INC.
2508 S. Grand Ave. E.
Springfield, IL 62703
(800) 826-4132, (217) 528-5636
Fax: (217) 528-8722

Wood sign panels with smooth vinyl surface for hand- or screen-printed lettering or applied vinyl lettering. Also offers fiberglass surfaced sign panels.

*SCOTT SIGN SYSTEMS
P.O. Box 1047
Tallevast, FL 34270
(800) 237-9447, (813) 355-5171
Fax: (813) 351-1787

A wide range of sign-making materials including a full line of letters and sign blanks. Also makes interior signs to client specifications.

SEPP LEAF PRODUCTS, INC.
381 Park Ave. S.
New York, NY 10016
(800) 971-7377, (212) 683-2840
Fax: (212) 725-0308

Gold leaf and related supplies. Also offers instructional video and technical assistance.

SIGN-MART
410 W. Flecher
Orange, CA 92665
(800) 533-9099, (714) 998-9470
Fax: (714) 998-6925

Blank vinyl banner material sold by the foot for hand- or silkscreen lettering.

TARA MATERIALS, INC.
P.O. Box 646
Lawrenceville, GA 30246
(800) 241-8129, (404) 963-5256
Fax: (404) 963-1044

Vinyl banner cloth in a variety of types and sizes. Also has ready-made banners.

TRADEMARK SIGN SYSTEMS
4 Hall Rd.
Ithaca, NY 14850
(800) 423-6895, (607) 423-6895
Fax: (607) 347-6645

Wood sign blanks for carving and sandblasting.

YARDER MANUFACTURING CO.
708 Phillips Ave.
Toledo, OH 43612
(419) 476-3933
Fax: (419) 478-6886

Sign blanks in steel and aluminum.

SIGN FABRICATORS

There are many kinds of signs, and the companies that fabricate and install them sometimes deal exclusively with a particular type of sign. The following listing of sign makers has been divided into six sections: Signage Systems, Banners, Electrical Signage, Electronic Message Boards, Porcelain Enamel Signs and Other. For more information about what's included, see the description under each of these category headings. Note: Firms preceded by an asterisk (*) are members of the Society of Environmental Graphic Designers (SEGD). For more information on this organization, see the listing in chapter thirteen under Graphic Arts Organizations.

SIGNAGE SYSTEMS

Signs that guide people through an environment (industry jargon refers to this as "wayfinding") must comply with codes and regulations. Whether the signage system is for a building or an office park, the signs for these applications must also maintain a degree of uniformity, and because there are usually many different signs involved, signage systems involve a lot of management—from the manufacture of each sign to the final installation. The companies that specialize in signage systems and their components are a special breed. Some of the companies in this category specialize in an aspect of signage systems, whereas others can handle all aspects of an entire project. Check individual listings or call to see how broad a fabricator's capabilities are.

*APCO
388 Grant St., SE
Atlanta, GA 30312
(404) 688-9000

Changeable signs and letter boards for building directories.

*ASI SIGN SYSTEMS
3890 W. Northwest Hwy., Ste. 102
Dallas, TX 75220
(800) ASI-SPEC (call for a local affiliate)
Fax: (214) 352-9741

Manufacturer of architectural interior and exterior signage systems. Also offers modular sign systems

TIP

In the dark about signage types and materials? *HOW* magazine's February, 1994, issue, dedicated to environmental graphics, offers many articles useful to graphic designers trying to expand from print into environmental graphics.

and updateable signs for directories and other applications. Thirty-eight affiliates in the U.S., Canada and United Kingdom.

*CARTER-MIOT
1829 Shop Rd.
P.O. Box 212
Columbia, SC 29202-0212

Fabricator and installer of interior and exterior architectural signage systems. Also provides project management.

*CHARLESTON INDUSTRIES, INC.
955 Estes Ave.
Elk Grove Village, IL 60007
(800) 722-0209, (708) 228-9096
Fax: (708) 956-7968

Custom and stock, interchangeable signs. Also interior directional information signage.

HOWARD INDUSTRIES
4985 Pittsburgh Ave.
Erie, PA 16509
(800) 458-0591, (814) 833-7000
Fax: (814) 838-0011

Exterior aluminum post and panel signage systems. Includes traffic controllers.

MCCURDY SHEA
10117 Princess Palm Ave., Ste. 100
Tampa, FL 33610
(813) 623-6398

Specializes in point-of-purchase and custom signage systems for retail.

*NORDQUIST SIGN CO., INC.
312 W. Lake St.
Minneapolis, MN 55408
(612) 823-7291
Fax: (612) 824-6211

Interior and exterior custom signs of all types (including electrical). Also specializes in signage systems.

SACHS LAWLOR
1717 S. Acoma St.
Denver, CO 80223
(800) 278-7771, (303) 777-7771
Fax: (303) 778-7175

Raised lettering and braille signage made from glass and Plexiglas™.

TIP

Need camera-ready art for the standard sign symbols that were developed for the U.S. Department of Transportation? You can buy a portfolio of fifty symbols along with their guidelines. Contact: ST Publications, 407 Gilbert Ave., Cincinnati, OH 45202; (800) 925-1110.

*SCOTT SIGN SYSTEMS
P.O. Box 1047
Tallevast, FL 34270
(800) 237-9447, (813) 355-5171
Fax: (813) 351-1787

Directory signage, interior signage systems. Also offers sign-making supplies and custom signs.

SETON IDENTIFICATION PRODUCTS
P.O. Box 3B-1331
New Haven, CT 06505
(800) 243-6624, (203) 488-8059
Fax: (800) 345-7819

Indoor/outdoor signs with universal graphic symbols. Includes parking, exit and pedestrian signs in vinyl on aluminum, engraved acrylic and more. Also offers changeable letter boards, identification badges and metal nameplates.

SPANDEX USA
1857 Walnut St.
Allentown, PA 18105
(800) 331-1891, (215) 434-9889

Modular sign systems to customer specifications.

BANNERS

Your local yellow pages will probably list some banner manufacturers. If your design uses standard typefaces and conventional materials, they will most likely be able to accommodate you. If their materials or banner sizes don't meet your needs, the companies listed here offer a wide range of possibilities.

BANNER CREATIONS
1433 E. Franklin Ave.
Minneapolis, MN 55404
(800) 326-3524, (612) 871-1015
Fax: (612) 871-0058

Manufactures in vinyl and cloth from supplied art or digital files. No limit in size.

CREATIVE BANNER
1700 Franey Blvd.
Minneapolis, MN 55430
(800) 528-8846, (612) 556-1118
Fax: (612) 566-8031

Paints and screen prints on nylon, vinyl, paper and other materials. Works from customer-furnished artwork as well as digital files.

*FABRIC ARTWORKS INTERNATIONAL
800 W. 9th St.
Little Rock, AR 72201
(800) 445-0653, (501) 375-7633
Fax: (501) 375-7638

Custom banners and flags.

*FLAGRAPHICS
30 Cross St.
Sommerville, MA 02145
(800) 323-9015, (617) 776-7549

Banners, textile signs and murals.

TARA MATERIALS, INC.
P.O. Box 646
Lawrenceville, GA 30246
(800) 241-8129, (404) 963-5256
Fax: (404) 963-1044

Ready-made banners as well as vinyl banner cloth in a variety of types and sizes.

ELECTRICAL SIGNAGE

You can find many local sign shops that will manufacture and maintain neon and back-lit electrical signage, but the companies listed below are nationally known. If your signage needs go beyond regional installation, some of these sign fabricators can handle installation and maintenance from coast to coast. Check individual listings.

*ARTKRAFT STRAUSS
830 12th Ave.
New York, NY 10001
(212) 265-5155

Custom neon creations.

*COLLINS SIGNS
P.O. Box 1253
Dothan, AL 36302
(205) 983-6518
Fax: (205) 983-1379

Fabricator and installer of primarily free-standing exterior signage. Includes back-lit electrical and neon.

*FEDERAL SIGN
140 E. Tower Dr.
Burr Ridge, IL 60521
(708) 565-2500
Fax: (708) 887-1183

Manufacturer and installer of custom electric signs. Handles primarily large-scale signage for interior and exterior applications, including neon.

*METROMEDIA TECHNOLOGIES
1320 N. Wilton Pl.
Los Angeles, CA 90028
(800) 433-4668, (213) 856-6500

Back-lit signs imprinted with computer-generated imagery and graphics.

MULHOLLAND HARPER CO.
24778 Meeting House Rd.
Denton, MD 21629
(800) 882-3052, (410) 469-1300
Fax: (410) 479-0207

Exterior illuminated signage.

NORDQUIST SIGN CO., INC.
312 W. Lake St.
Minneapolis, MN 55408
(612) 823-7291
Fax: (612) 824-6211

Interior and exterior back-lit electrical and neon signs.

PLASTI-LINE, INC.
13489 Slover Ave., Bldg. 7
Fontana, CA 92337
(909) 823-1239
Fax: (909) 823-2013

Manufacture, installation and maintenance of outdoor illuminated signage.

*SCOTT SIGN SYSTEMS
P.O. Box 1047
Tallevast, FL 34270
(800) 237-9447, (813) 355-5171
Fax: (813) 351-1787

Custom interior neon signs. Also offers sign-making supplies and signage systems.

UNIVERSAL SIGN CORP.
120 Dunbar Ave.
Oldsmar, FL 34677
(800) 784-SIGN, (813) 855-5400
Fax: (813) 855-9290

Builder and installer of illuminated signage and displays.

ELECTRONIC MESSAGE BOARDS

These companies manufacture the large-scale computer-controlled message boards that are incorporated into many exterior signs. They can also handle interior applications.

DATATRONIC CONTROL, INC.
5130 Dexham Rd.
Rowlett, TX 75088
(800) 527-1229, (214) 475-7879
Fax: (214) 475-4163

MULTIMEDIA
3300 Monier Circle, Ste. 150
Rancho Cordova, CA 95742
(800) 888-3007, (916) 852-4220
Fax: (916) 852-8325

TIME-O-MATIC, INC.
1015 Maple St.
P.O. Box 850
Danville, IL 61832
(800) 637-2645, (217) 442-0611
Fax: (217) 442-1020

UNITEC
34 Main St.
Whitesboro, NY 13492
(800) 383-6060, (315) 736-3967
Fax: (315) 736-4058

PORCELAIN ENAMEL SIGNS

Porcelain enamel on steel offers a wide range of colors and artistic detailing that can only be equalled by painted signage. However, the long-term, fade-resistant durability of porcelain enamel signs goes far beyond that of other types of signage.

*ELECTROMARK CO.
W. Port Bay Rd.
P.O. Box 25
Wolcott, NY 14590
(315) 594-8085

*FIREFORM PORCELAIN ENAMEL
368 Yolanda Ave.
Santa Rosa, CA 95404
(800) 643-3181, (707) 523-0580

*PG BELL/ENAMELTEC
60 Armstrong Ave.
Georgetown, Ontario L7G 4R9
Canada
(800) 663-8543 (U.S.)
(905) 873-1677

*PIONEER PORCELAIN ENAMEL CO., INC.
5531 Airport Way S.
Seattle, WA 98108
(206) 762-7540

*WINDSOR CORP.
312 Columbia St., NW
Olympia, WA 98501
(800) 824-7506, (206) 786-8200
Fax: (206) 786-6631

OTHER

A.R.K. RAMOS
P.O. Box 26388
Oklahoma City, OK 73126
(800) 725-7266, (405) 235-5505
Fax: (405) 232-8516

Specializes in cast-bronze, brass and aluminum letters and plaques.

ALD DECAL MANUFACTURING
435 Cleveland Ave., NW
Canton, OH 44702
(216) 453-2882
Fax: (216) 453-4313

Makes pressure-sensitive decals from customer-furnished art, photos and transparencies. Decals can be used on vehicles and other three-dimensional applications.

*BELSINGER SIGN WORKS, INC.
1300 Bayard St.
Baltimore, MD 21230
(800) 428-8848

Custom signage (primarily exterior). Illuminated, fabricated from metal and other materials.

*CORNELIUS ARCHITECTURAL PRODUCTS
30 Pine St.
Pittsburgh, PA 15223
(800) 553-7722, (412) 781-9003
Fax: (412) 871-7840

Custom signs from metal.

*CREATIVE EDGE CORP.
601 S. 23rd St.
Fairfield, IA 51556
(800) 394-8145, (515) 472-8145
Fax: (515) 472-2848

Waterjet fabricator of signs and architectural elements. Specializes in cutting and finishing of hard-to-shape materials such as stainless steel, stone, glass and brass.

*GOLDMAN ARTS
107 S. St., Ste. 403
Boston, MA 02111
(617) 423-6606
Fax: (617) 423-6601

Large-scale inflatable sculptures manufactured from nylon. Interior and exterior applications. Fabricates from customer specifications and also offers stock items such as bows and stars as well as various lengths of inflatable color tubing.

*NELSON-HARKINS
5301 N. Kedzie Ave.
Chicago, IL 60625
(800) 882-8989, (312) 478-6243
Fax: (312) 478-8227

Custom exterior signage from a wide range of materials (non-illuminated), some interior signage.

*NORDQUIST SIGN CO., INC.
312 W. Lake St.
Minneapolis, MN 55408
(612) 823-7291
Fax: (612) 824-6211

Interior and exterior custom signs of all types (including electrical). Specializes in signage systems.

P&D POLYGRAPHICS, INC.
823 Manatee Ave., W.
Bradenton, FL 34205
(813) 748-5510
Fax: (813) 747-8188

Simulated cast-bronze signage and plaques.

*PANNIER GRAPHICS
1239 Oak Rd.
Gibsonia, PA 15044
(412) 265-4900

Custom and stock fiberglass signs.

*SCOTT SIGN SYSTEMS
P.O. Box 1047
Tallevast, FL 34270
(800) 237-9447, (813) 355-5171
Fax: (813) 351-1787

Custom sandblasted, screen printed, etched and cast-metal signs.

UNITEX
521 Roosevelt Ave.
Central Falls, RI 02683
(401) 729-1100
Fax: (401) 729-1287

Backlit awnings for indoor and outdoor use. Available in sixteen colors. Call the following regional offices for a supplier in your area: Unitex South, (800) 759-0890; Unitex East, (800) 556-7254; Unitex West, (800) 456-6282; Unitex Midwest, (800) 843-6236; Unitex Southwest, (800) 433-5000.

FORMED LETTERS AND CUSTOM GRAPHICS

Formed letters and graphics can be used on flush-mounted signs. (Flush mounted signs are those that require attaching letters directly onto a surface—one of many ways signs can be created directly on walls, doors, posts, etc.) The following companies specialize in letters and graphics that can be flush mounted.

ADMART INTERNATIONAL
Goose Pike at Stanford Rd.
Danville, KY 40422
(800) 354-2101, (606) 236-7600
Fax: (606) 236-9050

Custom-crafted letterforms, logos, signage and display graphics from foam core board, Plexiglas™ and other materials.

EARL MICH CO.
806 N. Peoria St.
Chicago, IL 60622
(800) 642-4872, (312) 829-1552
Fax: (312) 829-5878

Vinyl and reflective sign letters and universal symbols. Produces custom graphics and logos from digital files. Also offers alphabet sheets, static lettering, dimensional letters, magnetic sheeting and more.

Goldman Arts specializes in inflatable sculptures. Many, such as this snail climbing up the wall of Boston's South Station, are on a gargantuan scale. For more information, see the Goldman Arts listing on page 69.

GEMINI INC.
103 Mensing Way
Cannon Falls, MN 55009
(800) 538-8377, (507) 263-3957
Fax: (507) 263-4887

Injection-molded plastic products, letters of vacuum-formed plastic. Also offers cast aluminum and bronze letters, aluminum and bronze plaques, custom metal cutouts, custom-formed plastic and edge trim gemlite letters.

IMAGEWEST
0-14122 Ironwood Dr., NW
Grand Rapids, MI 49504
(800) 359-6419, (616) 677-2300
Fax: (616) 677-2304

Converts clients' Macintosh or PC files into lettering and graphics in foam, metal, acrylic, wood, laminates, vinyls and other materials.

*SIMPLE SPACE-RITE
3315 W. Vernon
P.O. Box 11978
Phoenix, AZ 85061
(800) 528-8429, (602) 233-9483
Fax: (800) 329-9489

Custom letters and graphics from pressure-sensitive vinyl. Offers over eleven hundred typestyles.

SPANJER BROTHERS, INC.
1160 N. Howe St.
Chicago, IL 60610
(800) SPANJER, (312) 664-8000
Fax: (312) 664-7879

Letters in a wide selection of styles and sizes and a variety of colors and finishes. Formed from plastic, wood, cast aluminum and fabricated metal. Also has stock signs.

LARGE-SCALE IMAGING AND GRAPHICS

The following companies offer blow-ups of customer-supplied art and transparencies, including customer-furnished computer files on disk. The process used depends on the company, but may include electrostatic, ink jet and computerized airbrush. Large-scale imaging is used widely for billboards, vehicle graphics, display and other purposes. Prices vary according to the sub-strate and type of image. Check to find out which process is most cost-efficient for your needs.

AD GRAPHICS
6601 Lyons Rd., Ste. C-11
Coconut Creek, FL 33073
(800) 645-5740, (305) 421-4669
Fax: (305) 420-5929

Electrostatic printing on adhesive-backed vinyl. Can work from customer-furnished images, Mac- and PC-compatible files.

ALD DECAL MANUFACTURING
435 Cleveland Ave., NW
Canton, OH 44702
(216) 453-2882
Fax: (216) 453-4313

Offers large-scale imaging on pressure-sensitive decals from translucent Scotchcal™ (for back-lit applications) and Scotchlite™ reflective film. Works from customer-furnished art, photos and transparencies.

CACTUS SYSTEMS
P.O. Box 2077
Chino, CA 92708-2077
(909) 628-3265
Fax: (909) 628-0949

Electrostatic and ink jet printing on adhesive-back, reflective and translucent vinyl as well as paper.

DIGITABLE DIRIGIBLE
417 Canal St.
New York, NY 10013
(212) 431-1925
Fax: (212) 431-1978

Electrostatic printing on paper. Can work with customer furnished art as well as Mac-compatible computer files.

DIMENSIONAL IMPRESSIONS
4717 Van Nuys Blvd.
Sherman Oaks, CA 91403
(800) 964-7529, (818) 379-7039
Fax: (818) 379-7041

Ink-jet imaging on vinyl, paper, foam board and other surfaces. Process suitable for interior usage. Will work from transparencies, Mac- or PC-compatible files.

*GREGORY, INC.
200 S. Regier St.
P.O. Box 410
Buhler, KS 67522
(800) 835-2221, (316) 543-6657
Fax: (800) 835-2221, (316) 543-2690

Scotchprint™ graphics from supplied artwork, Mac and PC electronic files. Can print on paper, reflective, clear and transluscent substrates.

LOWEN COLOR GRAPHICS
1330 E. 4th St.
P.O. Box 1528
Hutchinson, KS 67504-1528
(800) 835-2365, (316) 663-2161
Fax: (316) 663-1429

Utilizes Scotchprint™ technology. Available on opaque, reflective and translucent vinyl films.

*MERRITT COLOR IMAGING
650 Franklin Ave.
Hartford, CT 06114
(800) 344-4477, (203) 296-2500
Fax: (203) 296-0414

Scotchprint™ imaging from transparencies, photos or digital files onto adhesive-backed vinyl.

MICHELANGELO SYSTEMS
Belcom Corp.
3135 Madison St.
Bellwood, IL 60104
(708) 544-4499
Fax: (708) 544-5607

Ink-jet process that can print an image on virtually any substrate, including carpet.

MIRATEC SYSTEMS, INC.
666 Transfer Rd.
St. Paul, MN 55114
(800) 336-1224, (612) 645-8440
Fax: (612) 645-8435

Scotchprint™ imaging from transparencies, photos or digital files.

NSP CORPORATE GRAPHICS
475 N. Daen Rd.
Auburn, AL 36830
(800) 876-6002
Fax: (205) 821-6919

Large-scale graphics on a variety of substrates using the Scotchprint™ electrostatic system.

ONYX GRAPHICS
6915 S. High Tech Dr.
Midvale, UT 84047
(800) 828-0723, (801) 568-9900
Fax: (801) 568-9911

Uses ink-jet process to print on high-gloss paper. Will laminate for increased durability.

SUNGRAF
325 W. Ansin Blvd.
Hallandale, FL 33009
(800) 327-1530, (305) 456-8500
Fax: (305) 454-2266

Digital airbrushed images in sizes up to sixteen feet high; unlimited lengths. Mac- and PC-compatible.

VISION GRAPHIC TECHNOLOGIES, INC.
2560 W. Directors Row
Salt Lake City, UT 84104
(800) 424-2483, (801) 973-8929
Fax: (801) 973-8944

SIGN-MAKING SOFTWARE

The following programs aid in the production of sign-making and large-scale imaging. Note: Information in this section is up-to-date at the time of this writing, but because software is consistently updated and new versions issued, be sure to contact each company to check on the current capability of the following programs and their compatibility with other programs.

DESIGN ART
ANAgraph, Inc.
3100 Pullman St.
Costa Mesa, CA 92626
(800) 942-4270, (714) 540-2400
Fax: (714) 966-2400

Creates type and graphic effects. Supports most sign-cutting plotters and color printers. PC-compatible. Operates under Microsoft Windows.

FLEXISIGN-PRO
Amiable Technologies
Scott Plaza 2, Ste., 625
Philadelphia, PA 19113-1518
(800) 229-9068, (215) 521-6300
Fax: (215) 521-0111

Mac- and PC-compatible sign-making software. Works with scanned images and images created in

TIP

For help in understanding the differences between the various types of large-format imaging services available, check out the following article: "A Giant Step," by Sean O'Leary, *Identity* magazine, May/June, 1994.

other programs to drive cutters and plotters for sign-making.

LETTER-ART
Symbol Graphics
1047 W. 6th St.
Corona, CA 91720
(909) 736-4040
Fax: (909) 737-0652

PC-compatible software for sign making. Allows for type creation, image editing and special graphic effects.

POSTERWORKS
1 Kendall Sq.
Building 600, Ste. 323
Cambridge, MA 02139
(617) 338-2222
Fax: (617) 338-2223

Aids in the design and production of large-format jobs such as posters, exhibits and displays up to ten thousand square feet. Macintosh compatible.

SEQUENCE PROGRAMMER
Logixx
433 Park Point Dr., Ste. 200
Golden, CO 80401
(800) 523-6989, (303) 526-5440
Fax: (303) 526-1558

Translates files from design software to drive plotters and cutters. Transfers from CorelDRAW and programs that can be interpreted by CorelDRAW.

SIGNPOST
Taylored Graphics
P.O. Box 1900
Freedom, CA 95019
(813) 948-7808

Linking software that drives cutters. Translates PostScript files created in Adobe Illustrator, Altsys FreeHand, Broderbund TypeStyler and other Mac-compatible programs.

business-to-business directory or yellow pages in your area for stock and custom-designed trade show booths and point-of-purchase displays.

ABEX DISPLAY SYSTEMS
71-1 Fair Ave.
N. Hollywood, CA 91605
(818) 764-5126
Fax: (818) 503-9955

Portable trade show displays. Call number above for a local distributor.

MADDOCKS & CO.
2011 Pontius Ave.
Los Angeles, CA 90025
(310) 477-4227

Specializes in point-of-sale merchandising displays.

M.D. ENTERPRISES DISPLAY SYSTEMS
4907 W. Hanover Ave.
Dallas, TX 75209
(214) 352-2802

Displays made of fabric panels, knock-down panels and tubular construction.

SKYLINE DISPLAY, INC.
12345 Portland Ave. S.
Burensville, MN 55337
(612) 895-6375, (800) 328-2725
Fax: (612) 895-6391

Portable trade show displays.

THE UNITED GROUP
9700 Frontage Rd.
South Gate, CA 90280
(213) 927-7741

Designer and manufacturer of high-impact displays. Handles point-of-purchase and trade show displays.

POINT-OF-PURCHASE DISPLAYS AND TRADE SHOW BOOTHS

The following companies produce display booths. Some of these national manufacturers also make their products available through local vendors. Also check the

DISPLAY ITEMS AND SUPPLIES

These companies offer components that can be useful in displaying items or putting together a trade show booth. Note: Firms preceded by an asterisk (*) are members of the Society of Environmental Graphic Designers (SEGD). For more information on this organization, see the listing in chapter thirteen, under Graphic Arts Organizations.

A.I.M. DISPLAYS
P.O. Box 718
Franklin, NC 28734
(800) 524-9833

Aluminum display panels with folding hinges. Available in a variety of sizes.

CREATIVE ENERGIES INC.
1609 N. Magnolia Ave.
Ocala, FL 34475
(904) 351-8889

Public hanging systems comprised of stackable panels. Company also makes canopies.

DEALERS SUPPLY
P.O. Box 717
Matawan, NJ 07747
(800) 524-0576

Display supplies, including table covers, showcases, canopies, folding tables, booth signs, lighting, security aids and more.

PANELS BY PAITH
Rte. 6, Box 656
Roxboro, NC 27573
(800) 67-PAITH, (910) 599-3437
Fax: (910) 599-8827

Plaques in several shapes and sizes. Bases and glass domes for display of individual items.

*SCOTT SIGN SYSTEMS
P.O. Box 1047
Tallevast, FL 34270
(800) 237-9447, (813) 355-5171
Fax: (813) 351-1787

Acrylic brochure racks, light boxes and more.

RESTAURANT-RELATED ITEMS

Chapter

RESTAURANT

AND

HOSPITALITY

INDUSTRY

ITEMS

menus

MENU LAMINATING

These companies will laminate preprinted menus to provide extra durability. Check individual listings for minimum quantities. If you're interested in clear, vinyl sleeves that can be reused, see the listings in this chapter under Restaurant Supplies and Furnishings (pages 77-78).

ACCUPRINT & LAMINATING OF CINCINNATI
49 E. 4th St.
Cincinnati, OH 45202
(513) 651-1078
Fax: (513) 651-5624

CAULASTICS
5955 Mission St.
Daly City, CA 94014
(415) 585-9600
Fax: (415) 585-5209

CENTURY PLUS
2701 Girard, NE
Albuquerque, NM 87107
(505) 888-2901
Fax: (505) 888-2902

COMMERCIAL LAMINATING CO.
3131 Chester Ave.
Cleveland, OH 44114
(216) 781-2434
Fax: (216) 781-9413

D&E VINYL CORP.
13524 Vintage Pl.
Chino, CA 91710
(800) 929-2148, (909) 590-0502
Fax: (909) 591-7822

G2 GRAPHIC SERVICE, INC.
7014 Sunset Blvd.
Los Angeles, CA 90028
(213) 467-7828
(818) 845-8333 (pick-up and delivery)
Fax: (213) 469-0381

INTERNATIONAL LAMINATING
1712 Springfield St.
Dayton, OH 45403
(513) 254-8181
Fax: (513) 256-8813

LAMINATING SERVICES CO.
7359 Varna Ave.
North Hollywood, CA 91605
(818) 982-9065, (213) 460-4104
Fax: (818) 982-2787

PAVLIK LAMINATING
3418 S. 48th St., #8
Phoenix, AZ 85040
(602) 968-4601
Fax: (602) 968-6422

SUPERIOR REPROGRAPHICS
1925 5th Ave.
Seattle, WA 98101
(206) 443-6900
Fax: (206) 441-8390

SIGNAGE

These companies specialize in custom and stock interchangeable signage systems, suitable for over-the-counter and freestanding letter boards where menu changes and specials can be posted on a day-to-day basis. For additional signage needs, check the other listings under Sign Fabricators in chapter six.

APCO
388 Grant St., SE
Atlanta, GA 30312
(404) 688-9000

ASI SIGN SYSTEMS
3890 W. Northwest Hwy., Ste. 102
Dallas, TX 75220
(800) ASI-SPEC (call for a local affiliate)
Fax: (214) 352-9741

CHARLESTON INDUSTRIES, INC.
955 Estes Ave.
Elk Grove Village, IL 60007
(800) 722-0209, (708) 228-9096
Fax: (708) 956-7968

SETON IDENTIFICATION PRODUCTS
P.O. Box 3B-1331
New Haven, CT 06505
(800) 243-6624, (203) 488-8059
Fax: (800) 345-7819

APPAREL

These companies can supply aprons, chef's hats and uniforms appropriate for restaurant personnel. For custom garment printing in a more casual mode (T-shirts, polo shirts, etc.), check out listings for Garment Printers in chapter eight.

ANCHORTEX CORP.
1304 Marlkress Rd.
P.O. Box 3731
Cherry Hill, NJ 08003
(609) 768-5240
Fax: (609) 768-5547

Offers stock uniforms for waiters, waitresses and kitchen personnel, including chef's coats, hats and aprons.

ATLAS UNIFORM CO.
5943 W. Lawrence, Dept. TR
Chicago, IL 60630
(800) 635-3578, (312) 725-1220
Fax: (312) 725-6191

Offers stock and custom designs for waiters', waitresses' and chef's clothes (including aprons), as well as T-shirts and jackets. Offers career apparel.

FIRST CLASS HOTEL & RESTAURANT SUPPLY
21-T Marlboro Dr.
Port Jefferson Station, NY 11776
(800) 587-6146, (516) 476-1534
Fax: (516) 476-1543

Offers apparel for kitchen personnel and servers, including aprons, uniforms and chef's hats. All can be screen printed or embroidered with customer-furnished artwork. Also carries other restaurant supplies.

TEXTILE MANUFACTURING
8111 Garden Rd.
Riviera Beach, FL 33404
(800) 262-7247, (800) 323-0054
Fax: (407) 844-4148

Cloth bib aprons starting as low as $2.95 each. Company will screen print and embroider aprons to customer specifications.

TKO
2740 White Oak
Lawn Lake, MN 55356
(800) 347-8TKO

Offers many styles of cloth aprons for cooks, servers, etc. Will screen print and embroider to customer specifications. Advertises no minimums.

RESTAURANT SUPPLIES AND FURNISHINGS

These manufacturers offer a variety of restaurant items that can be custom fabricated to your specifications or printed with your designs.

BOXERBRAND
423 W. Broadway
Boston, MA 02127
(800) 253-2772
Fax: (617) 464-4401

Makes vinyl menu covers. Offers deluxe and economy styles.

BUFFALO CHINA
658 Bailey Ave.
Buffalo, NY 14206
(800) 828-7033, (716) 824-2378

Custom and stock designs in china dinnerware. Items can be printed with customer-furnished designs. Also offers in-house design service.

COMPETITIVE EDGE
2711 Grand Ave.
Des Moines, IA 50312
(800) 458-3343, (515) 280-3343
Fax: (515) 288-3343

Offers custom-imprinted napkins, matches, stir-sticks and other specialty items.

CONTINENTAL/SILITE INTERNATIONAL
P.O. Box 53006
Oklahoma City, OK 73152-3006
(800) 654-8210
Fax: (405) 528-6338

Manufactures plastic color-coordinated dinnerware, deli displays and trays custom-fabricated and printed to client specifications.

DECOR CONCEPTS
5611 Peck Rd.
Arcadia, CA 91006
(800) 959-0136
Fax: (818) 444-4536

Specializes in modular furniture for cafeterias, food courts and fast-food restaurants. Offers a variety of designs and finishes in counters, counter-tops and stools, tables and chairs, etc. Offers products for indoor and outdoor use.

FIRST CLASS HOTEL & RESTAURANT SUPPLY
21-T Marlboro Dr.
Port Jefferson Station, NY 11776
(800) 587-6146, (516) 476-1534
Fax: (516) 476-1543

Offers china and plastic dinnerware, paper and plastic cups and other containers, paper and cloth napkins and tablecloths and other items, including kitchen apparel and aprons. All can be printed or embroidered to customer specifications.

GUEST CHECKS AMERICA
2785 Kurtz St., #12
San Diego, CA 92110
(800) 487-4478
Fax: (619) 298-4472

Offers vinyl menu covers in single-, two- or three-panel configurations. Also offers custom-printed matches and guest checks.

JAMES RIVER CORP.
Commercial Products Division
800 Connecticut Ave.
Norwalk, CT 06856-6000
(800) 257-9744, (203) 854-2000

Manufactures blank and printed dinner, beverage and dispenser napkins. Also makes paper and plastic cups and other paper and plastic containers with lids.

NOVELTY CRYSTAL CORP.
21005 O'Brien Rd.
Groveland, FL 34736
(800) 429-9037, (904) 429-9036
Fax: (904) 429-9039

Offers blank and custom-imprinted plastic stemware, mugs and tumblers. Many styles available in a variety of colors.

ORA/CARR TEXTILES
311 Park Ave., SE
Atlanta, GA 30312
(800) 533-2810
Fax: (404) 522-1887

Manufactures cloth napkins.

OSWALT MENU CO., INC.
1474 S. State Rd. 3
Hartford City, IN 47438
(800) 822-6368
Fax: (317) 348-3137

Makes menu covers with plastic sleeves for inserts. Offers Lexhide or custom-printed covers, spiral binding or folded covers.

PAPER ART CO., INC.
7240 Shadeland Way, Ste. 300
Indianapolis, IN 46256
(317) 841-9999

Manufactures printed and embossed paper napkins.

PLASTICRAFTERS
331 Market St.
Warren, RI 02885
(800) 572-2194, (401) 247-0392

Makes tabletop display stands for specials. Offers clear plastic single-, double- and tri-panel configurations in a variety of sizes and styles.

RAY'S BOOTHS
2444 W. 21st St.
Chicago, IL 60608
(800) 49-BOOTH, (312) 523-3355

Custom designed and upholstered booths and other restaurant furniture. Includes counters, cabinets, booths, chairs, stools and bookshelves.

TWEEL HOME FURNISHINGS, INC.
900-T Passaic Ave.
Harrison, NJ 07029
(800) 273-6308
Fax: (201) 481-1911

Makes tablecloths stitched and imprinted to customer specifications.

GARMENTS AND UNIFORMS

Chapter

PRINTED

GARMENTS,

UNIFORMS

AND

ACCESSORIES

GARMENT PRINTERS BY REGION

These garment screen printers have appeared over the last two years in Impressions magazine's annual top one hundred list. Impressions is a trade publication for garment sceen printers and qualifies its annual top one hundred on average gross sales, number of impressions and number of pieces printed.

Items offered by these companies include T-shirts and polo shirts, sweatshirts, jackets, hats, tote bags, visors and more. In addition to screen printing, imprinting options include embroidery, appliqués, flocked imprints and more. Check individual listings for other imprinting options and minimum quantities.

EAST (CT, NH, MA, ME, RI, VT, DC, DE, MD, NJ, NY, PA)

AMPRO SPORTSWEAR
30 Bunting Ln.
Primos, PA 19018
(800) 341-4008
Fax: (610) 623-9000

APSCO ENTERPRISES
50th St. & 1st Ave.
Brooklyn, NY 11232
(718) 965-9500
Fax: (718) 965-3088

GEM GROUP, INC.
20 Locust St.
Danvers, MA 01930
(508) 774-0161
Fax: (508) 771-6283

OCEAN ATLANTIC TEXTILE PRINTING, INC.
502 S. Main St.
Cape May Court House, NJ 08210
(609) 465-2100
Fax: (609) 465-3856

OHIOPYLE PRINTS
RD. #1/Dinnerbell Rd.
Ohiopyle, PA 15470
(412) 329-4652
Fax: (412) 329-1001

R.C. SCREENPRINTING
501 River St.
Paterson, NJ 07524
(201) 742-7148
Fax: (201) 742-6480

SOUTH (AL, FL, GA, KY, LA, MS, NC, SC, TN, TX, VA, WV)

AMALGAMATED T-SHIRTS, INC.
200 Permalume Pl.
Atlanta, GA 30318
(404) 352-3660
Fax: (404) 352-5376

CARROUSEL PRODUCTIONS, INC.
11000 Wilcrest, Ste. 100
Houston, TX 77099
(713) 568-9300
Fax: (713) 568-9498

CHAMPION AWARDS, INC.
3649 Winplace Rd.
Memphis, TN 38118
(901) 365-4830
Fax: (901) 365-2796

THE DOE-SPUN GROUP
750 N. Pine St.
Rocky Mount, NC 27804
(919) 977-6353
Fax: (919) 985-2336

EBERT SPORTSWEAR, INC.
5000 Fernandina Rd.
Columbia, SC 29212
(803) 722-2752
Fax: (803) 772-6551

LONESTAR SPORTSWEAR/TIMOTHY BULL, INC.
2816 Shamrock Ave.
Fort Worth, TX 76107
(817) 332-7771
Fax: (817) 332-9110

LOUISIANA GARMENT SILK SCREENERS, INC.
1949 Lafayette St.
New Orleans, LA 70113
(504) 525-4000
Fax: (504) 522-3535

MAGNUM INDUSTRIES, INC.
7636 E. 46th St.
Tulsa, OK 74145
(918) 665-7636
Fax: (918) 665-7667

MENDEZ SPORTSWEAR
13000 NW 42nd Ave.
Miami, FL 33054
(305) 685-3490
Fax: (305) 687-1393

PM ENTERPRISES, INC.
300 Jacobson Dr.
Rock Branch Industrial Park
Poca, WV 25159
(304) 755-4191
Fax: (304) 755-8703

SILVERWING PRODUCTIONS, INC.
11210 Goodnight Ln.
Dallas, TX 75229
(214) 243-4396
Fax: (214) 243-4107

SPORTSGRAPHIC SERVICES, INC.
6235 S. Manhattan Ave.
Tampa, FL 33616
(813) 837-0572
Fax: (813) 831-6319

SPORTSWEAR PROMOTIONS, INC.
98 Belinda Pkwy.
P.O. Box 1137
Mt. Juliet, TN 37122
(615) 758-3033
Fax: (615) 758-5999

STANLEY MICHAELS, INC.
5280 NW 165th St.
Miami, FL 33014
(305) 621-0800
Fax: (305) 620-2666

T.B. RIDDLES, INC.
635 E. Durst Ave.
Greenwood, SC 29649
(803) 223-4964
Fax: (803) 229-4382

T.S. DESIGNS, INC.
2053 Willow Springs Ln.
Burlington, NC 27215
(910) 229-6426
Fax: (910) 226-4418

20/20 DESIGN, INC.
6257 Hwy. 76, E.
Springfield, TN 37172
(615) 384-1359
Fax: (615) 384-6193

MIDWEST (IA, IL, IN, MI, MN, MO, OH, WI)

BLAZER SCREENPRINT CO., INC.
3135 W. Grand Ave.
Chicago, IL 60622
(312) 638-2020
Fax: (312) 638-6388

CREATIVE SILKSCREEN & DESIGN, INC.
1100 Buchanan St.
Rockford, IL 61101
(815) 963-7733
Fax: (815) 963-7722

HOLOUBEK, INC.
W. 238 Rockwood Dr.
Waukesha, WI 53188
(414) 547-0500
Fax: (414) 547-5847

LSJ SPORTSWEAR, INC.
54 Golf Car Rd.
Deerfield, WI 53531
(608) 764-5425
Fax: (608) 764-5159

PRINTWORKS, INC.
5695 W. Franklin Dr.
Franklin, WI 53132-8606
(414) 421-5400
Fax: (414) 421-3970

SIGNAL ARTWEAR, INC.
570 S. Miami St.
Wabash, IN 46992
(219) 563-8302
Fax: (219) 563-1811

SUGAR CREEK DESIGNS, INC.
202 Joplin St.
Joplin, MO 64801
(417) 781-9696
Fax: (417) 781-6409

SUNBURST SPORTSWEAR
931 N. DuPage Ave.
Lombard, IL 60148
(708) 629-2700
Fax: (708) 629-8586

TNT IMPRINTED APPAREL, INC.
1500 Jackson St., NE
Minneapolis, MN 55413
(612) 788-9177
Fax: (612) 788-9178

WEST (CA, CO, KS, NB, ND, NV, SD, UT, WY)

ACTION SHIRTS
15606 Producer Ln.
Huntington Beach, CA 92649
(714) 891-1263
Fax: (714) 891-8592

AMERICAN MARKETING WORKS
14501 S. Figueroa
Gardena, CA 90248
(310) 515-7230
Fax: (310) 715-1507

ATLAS SPORTSWEAR, INC.
18529 E. Valley Hwy.
Keni, WA 98032
(206) 656-9111
Fax: (206) 656-9115

COLLEGIATE GRAPHICS
2901 S. Highland, 12B
Las Vegas, NV 89101
(702) 737-0771
Fax: (702) 737-8415

GLOBAL 2000, INC.
9852 Max Shapiro Way
S. El Monte, CA 91733
(818) 448-2000
Fax: (818) 448-2052

GOLDEN SQUEEGEE
900 Santa Fe Dr.
Denver, CO 80204
(303) 572-1164
Fax: (303) 572-1190

HABITAT
924 Spring Creek Rd.
Montrose, CO 81401
(303) 249-3333
Fax: (303) 249-0328

I-SCREEN OF CALIFORNIA
1388 E. 15th St.
Los Angeles, CA 90021
(213) 746-2008
Fax: (213) 746-7337

INSTA GRAPHICS SYSTEMS
13925 E. 166th St.
Cerritos, CA 90702
(310) 404-3000
Fax: (310) 404-3010

JUNGLE RAGS
43105 Business Park Dr.
Temecula, CA 92590
(909) 694-0093
Fax: (909) 694-8546

KOALA ARTS, INC.
3425 Hancock St.
San Diego, CA 92110
(619) 692-9400
Fax: (619) 692-9996

MCKIBBEN SCREEN PRINTING & DIST., INC.
1525 E. St. Gertrude Pl.
Santa Ana, CA 92705
(714) 754-1774
Fax: (714) 957-1402

MORNING SUN
3500-C 20th St., E.
Tacoma, WA 98424
(206) 922-6589
Fax: (206) 922-9440

NATIONAL GARMENT CO.
3928 Ross Ln.
Chanute, KS 66720
(316) 431-6411
Fax: (316) 431-3904

PACIFIC IMPRESSIONS
3535 De La Cruz Blvd.
Santa Clara, CA 95054
(408) 727-4200
Fax: (408) 988-2493

SUN SPORTSWEAR
6520 S. 190th St.
Kent, WA 98032
(206) 251-3565
Fax: (206) 251-0527

SWINGSTER
8257 Hedge Lane Terrace
Shawnee, KS 66227
(913) 441-2703
Fax: (913) 441-3541

T.B.P.C. INC.
235 S. 9th Ave.
Industry, CA 91744
(818) 968-2130
Fax: (818) 968-2679

UNIFORM AND ACCESSORIES SUPPLIERS

These manufacturers offer a variety of uniform types and imprint possibilities as well as other accessories. Check each listing for minimum orders as well as availability of silkscreen printing, embroidery and emblem application.

ANCHORTEX CORP.
1304 Marlkress Rd.
P.O. Box 3731
Cherry Hill, NJ 08003
(800) 221-9263, (609) 768-5240
Fax: (800) 221-9265

Offers stock uniforms for kitchen personnel, security, housekeeping, medical personnel and more, as well as career-look blazers and pants. Also stocks T-shirts and caps.

ANTLER UNIFORMS
34-01 38th Ave.
Long Island City, NY 11101
(800) 893-4027, (718) 361-2800
Fax: (718) 361-2680

Specializes in outerwear for security personnel, ground crews, delivery services and others.

APPARELMASTER
2786 E. Crescentville Rd.
Cincinnati, OH 45262
(800) 543-1678, (513) 772-7721
Fax: (513) 772-4117

Stock and custom designs for industrial, security, kitchen, housekeeping and career-look personnel.

If you're interested in learning more about garment printing, there are two trade magazines that can provide further insights into the garment printing industry. Impressions magazine is published monthly and covers textile screen printing as well as garment printing. Contact Impressions at 13760 Noel Rd., Ste. 500, Dallas, TX 75240; (800) 527-0207, (214) 419-7894. SCREENplay is a monthly magazine that focuses on imprinted sportswear. Contact SCREENplay at 407 Gilbert Ave., Cincinnati, OH 45202; (513) 421-2050.

ARAMARK UNIFORM SERVICES
115 N. 1st St.
Burbank, CA 91502
(800) 327-2839, (818) 973-3700
Fax: (800) 436-3132

Uniform designs for all kinds of personnel. Includes coveralls, aprons and smocks.

ATD-AMERICAN CO.
137 Greenwood Ave.
Wyncote, PA 19095-1396
(800) 523-2300, (215) 576-1000
Fax: (215) 576-1827

Specializes in a complete line of men's and women's underwear for government, institutions and retail.

ATLAS UNIFORM CO.
5943 W. Lawrence, Dept. TR
Chicago, IL 60630
(800) 635-3578, (312) 725-1220
Fax: (312) 725-6191

Offers stock and custom designs for industrial, security, institutional and promotional purposes. Includes aprons, career looks, medical garments, outerwear and sports gear.

DESANTIS HOLSTER & LEATHER GOODS
149 Denton Ave.
New Hyde Park, NY 11040
(516) 354-8000
Fax: (516) 354-7501

Specializes in uniform belts, holsters and batons.

FAWN INDUSTRIES, INC. (EAST COAST)
Hwy. 851
P.O. Box 230
New Park, PA 17352
(800) 388-3296, (717) 382-4855

Specializes in custom embroidery on jackets, polo shirts, T-shirts and other items.

FAWN INDUSTRIES, INC. (WEST COAST)
7650 New Castle Rd.
P.O. Box 30727
Stockton, CA 95213
(800) 388-3296, (209) 464-7777

Specializes in custom embroidery on jackets, polo shirts, T-shirts and other items.

FIRST CLASS HOTEL & RESTAURANT SUPPLY
21-T Marlboro Dr.
Port Jefferson Station, NY 11776
(800) 587-6146, (516) 476-1534
Fax: (516) 476-1543

Specializes in uniforms for food service, hotel lobby and recreation areas and housekeeping uniforms. Offers stock and custom designs.

GARMENT CORP. OF AMERICA
801 41st St.
Miami Beach, FL 33140
(800) 944-4300, (305) 531-4040
Fax: (800) 777-1015

Offers stock designs for industrial work clothes.

GEORGE GLOVE CO.
266 S. Dean St.
Englewood, NJ 07631-5209
(800) 631-4292, (201) 567-7500
Fax: (201) 567-0567

Offers all kinds of gloves in all sizes, colors and materials including parade gloves, waiters' gloves and work gloves.

JEDA TRADING CORP.
21-05 51st Ave.
Long Island City, NY 11101
(800) 229-8919, (718) 784-1166
Fax: (718) 784-7019

Offers stock uniforms for service and security personnel, including outerwear, as well as coordinated blazers, slacks, dress shirts, etc.

LEVENTHAL BROS. & CO., INC.
36 Maple Pl.
Manhasset, NY 11030
(800) 663-4965, (516) 365-9540
Fax: (516) 365-9547

Specialty is uniforms for security, law enforcement and industrial personnel.

MICHAEL'S UNIFORM COMPANY, INC.
7182 W. Grand Ave.
Chicago, IL 60635
(800) 828-0601, (312) 287-8700
Fax: (312) 287-3292

Industrial and career apparel. Includes smocks, coveralls, lab coats, jackets, windbreakers and more.

PEERLESS UNIFORM MANUFACTURING CO.
21600 Lassen St.
Chatsworth, CA 91311
(800) 842-4592, (818) 341-0700
Fax: (818) 341-1546

Custom and stock designs for industry, health care, food and other service industries.

SHIRTZ UNLIMITED
482 S. Griggs
St. Paul, MN 55116
(800) 728-4291, (612) 699-3847
Fax: (612) 699-3847

Offers sports team apparel, T-shirts, caps, polo shirts, sweatshirts and jackets.

SOME'S UNIFORMS, INC.
63 Rte. 17
Paramus, NJ 07652
(800) 631-7077, (201) 843-1199
Fax: (201) 843-3014

Specializes in career and professional uniforms for federal, state, county, security and industrial agencies and private industry in foreign countries.

SPEDMILL, INC.
1132 N. Carrolton Ave.
Baton Rouge, LA 70806
(800) 922-1463, (504) 924-1463
Fax: (504) 923-3225

Specializes in industrial uniforms.

TODD UNIFORMS FOR BUSINESS
3668 S. Geyer Rd.
St. Louis, MO 63127
(800) 325-9516, (314) 984-0365
Fax: (314) 984-5736

Offers stock and custom designs for all types of personnel. Emphasizes image building.

UNIFIRST
3047 E. Commerce
San Antonio, TX 78220
(800) 225-3364, (210) 222-8695

Stock and custom designs for industrial and medical personnel as well as career-look blazers and slacks. Emphasizes image building.

UNITOG
101 W. 11th
Kansas City, MO 64105
(800) 288-8707, (816) 474-7000

Manufactures all kinds of uniforms.

WEINTRAUB BROTHERS CO., INC.
2695 Philmont Ave.
Huntingdon Valley, PA 19006
(800) 355-1037, (215) 938-7540
Fax: (215) 938-7630

Emphasizes image building. Offers custom design service. Also offers military uniforms.

PATCHES AND EMBLEMS

These companies specialize in custom-embroidered uniform patches. Check individual listings for minimum quantities.

FAWN INDUSTRIES, INC.
Hwy. 851
P.O. Box 230
New Park, PA 17352
(800) 388-3296, (717) 382-4855

RECCO MAID EMBROIDERY CO.
4624 W. Cornelia Ave.
Chicago, IL 60641-3792
(800) 345-3458
Fax: (312) 286-0220

SWISS CRAFT EMBROIDERY CO., INC.
1601 N. Natchez Ave., Dept. 95
Chicago, IL 60635
(800) 835-4666
Fax: (312) 622-5308

CUSTOM IMPRINTED PRODUCTS

Chapter

9

SPECIALTY

ITEMS

THAT CAN

BE CUSTOM

PRINTED

watches

BINDERS AND FOLDERS

The following companies offer folders and binders that can be ordered preprinted with your graphics. For smaller orders, or to order blank folders that can be customized with preprinted pressure-sensitive labels, see the listings in chapter eleven, pages 110-111.

ADMORE
24707 Wood Ct.
Mt. Clemens, MI 48045
(800) 523-6673
Fax: (810) 949-8968

Custom presentation folders employing a number of processes: four-color, foil stamping, embossing and lamination.

AMERICAN THERMOPLASTIC CO.
106 Gama Dr., Ste. 599
Pittsburgh, PA 15238-9857
(800) 245-6600
Fax: (412) 967-9990

Custom-imprinted binders and index sets. Offers a free catalog.

CRESTLINE CO., INC.
22 W. 21st St.
New York, NY 10010
(800) 221-7797, (212) 741-3300
Fax: (212) 807-8290

Custom-imprinted pocket folders and binders. Offers free samples and a catalog.

FOLDER FACTORY
P.O. Box 429
Edinburg, VA 22824-0429
(800) 296-4321, (703) 984-9699

Manufactures custom-imprinted pocket folders. Offers a free catalog.

LABELS AND STICKERS

These companies will manufacture labels and stickers to customer specifications. For smaller quantities of pressure-sensitive labels, check your local business-to-business directory.

DANA LABELS, INC.
7778 SW Nimbus Ave.
Beaverton, OR 97005
(503) 646-7933

Garment labels and size tabs, pressure-sensitive labels, paper shipping labels and other types.

GRAPHCOMM SERVICES
P.O. Box 220
Freeland, WA 98249
(360) 331-5668
Fax: (360) 331-3282

Custom labels and self-inking stamps. Also offers custom hang-tags and tagging equipment.

STERLING NAME TAPE CO.
P.O. Box 110
Winsted, CT 06098
(203) 379-5142
Fax: (203) 379-0394

Manufactures custom clothing labels (in one or more ink colors) from polysatin.

PROMOTIONAL ITEMS AND MARKETING AIDS

The following companies offer a wide variety of custom-imprinted products. Contact each for their catalog to find out what the possibilities are.

AMSTER NOVELTY CO., INC.
75-13-T 31st Ave.
Middle Village, NY 11379
(800) 314-4067
Fax: (718) 326-4365

Drawstring pouches, totes and other bags. Custom imprints with hot stamping, silkscreening and embroidery. Stitches fabrics to customer specifications.

COMPETITIVE EDGE
2711 Grand Ave.
Des Moines, IA 50312
(800) 458-3343, (515) 280-3343
Fax: (515) 288-3343

Offers a variety of items including banners, imprinted pens and pencils, badges and pins, matches, napkins, etc., as well as a variety of garments. Can screen print products or embroider to customer specifications.

THE CORPORATE CHOICE

2369 Lincoln Ave.

Hayward, CA 94545

(800) 792-2277, (510) 786-1132

Fax: (510) 786-1111

Umbrellas, hats, shirts, pens, mugs, you name it. The Corporate Choice will also custom imprint unique items not included in its catalog.

CRESTLINE CO., INC.

22 W. 21st St.

New York, NY 10010

(800) 221-7797, (212) 741-3300

Fax: (212) 807-8290

Offers hundreds of items including badges, mugs, banners and pens.

LAPEL PIN, INC.

Dept. US

3609 Thousand Oaks Blvd., #222

Westlake Village, CA 91362

(800) 229-7467, (805) 374-1414

Fax: (805) 374-1417

Makes enamel pins from customer-furnished artwork.

LNS ENTERPRISES

946 Hope St., Ste. 157

Stamford, CT 06907-2203

(800) 648-3770

Fax: (800) 348-3770

T-shirts and sweatshirts, leather and vinyl items, desk accessories, mugs, executive gifts, gourmet gifts, etc.

MARTGUILD

576 Industrial Pkwy.

P.O. Box 382

Chagrin Falls, OH 44022-0382

(800) 245-8978, (216) 247-8978

Fax: (216) 247-1107

Custom-imprinted medals, key tags, jewelry, paperweights, belt buckles, etc. Offers a free catalog.

NELSON MARKETING

P.O. Box 320

Oshkosh, WI 54902-0320

(800) 5-IMPRINT

Fax: (414) 236-7282

Offers hats, tote bags, pens, desk accessories, mugs, executive gifts and more. Will send a free catalog.

PINSOURCE

Specialties Unlimited

1233 Shelburne Rd.

S. Burlington, VT 05403

(800) 678-9288

Fax: (802) 865-3777

Custom-designed lapel pins in cloisonne and enamel. Will send a free catalog.

SPECIALTIES UNLIMITED

1233 Shelburne Rd.

S. Burlington, VT 05403

(800) 678-9288

Fax: (802) 865-3777

Advertising specialties including paper weights, jewelry. Offers a free catalog.

SUCCESSORIES, INC.

919 Springer Dr.

Lombard, IL 60148

(800) 847-8144, (708) 953-2110

Fax: (708) 953-1229

Offers award and recognition items in brass and crystal, as well as other custom-imprinted products, including T-shirts (and other garments), mugs, hats, etc. Will send a free catalog.

WHIRLEY INDUSTRIES, INC.

618 4th Ave.

P.O. Box 988

Warren, PA 16365-4923

(800) 825-5575

Fax: (814) 723-3245

Custom-imprinted thermo and car mugs.

BADGES AND EMBLEMS

FAWN INDUSTRIES, INC.

Hwy. 851

P.O. Box 230

New Park, PA 17352

(800) 388-3296, (717) 382-4855

Specializes in embroidered patches.

JOHNSON'S

1208 Brooklands Rd.

Dayton, OH 45409

(800) 563-3919, (513) 294-5646

Aviation wings and police, medical and other insignias manufactured from metal.

RECCO MAID EMBROIDERY CO.
4624 W. Cornelia Ave.
Chicago, IL 60641-3792
(800) 345-3458
Fax: (312) 286-0220

Specializes in embroidered patches.

SWISS CRAFT EMBROIDERY CO., INC.
1601 N. Natchez Ave., Dept. 95
Chicago, IL 60635
(800) 835-4666
Fax: (312) 622-5308

Specializes in embroidered patches.

WATCHES

The following companies offer watches with faces that can be custom-imprinted with supplied art.

FASHION WATCH, INC.
2580 Corporate Place, #102-US10
Monterey Park, CA 91754
(800) 733-1332, (213) 881-9839
Fax: (213) 881-9819

Full-color logos and custom art on eight possible styles.

GREAT AMERICAN IMAGES
1 Water Park Dr., Ste. 213-US
San Mateo, CA 94403
(415) 358-0800
Fax: (415) 358-0543

Full-color logos and custom art on several styles.

IMAGE WATCHES, INC.
9095 Telstar Ave.
Elmonte, CA 91731-2809
(818) 312-2828
Fax: (818) 312-2851

Offers six different styles.

INFINITY WATCH CORP.
2530 Corporate Place, Ste. 110, Dept. US
Monterey Park, CA 91754
(800) 313-8808, (213) 266-0998
Fax: (213) 266-1115

Can print simple designs or full-color. Offers six different styles.

PERFECT TIME, INC.
1422-28 S. Broadway, Dept. US
Los Angeles, CA 90015
(800) 872-0392, (213) 746-3231
Fax: (213) 746-1169

Full-color logos and custom art on a variety of watch styles.

TIME DIMENSION, INC.
9528 Rush St., #D
South El Monte, CA 91733
(800) 988-5646, (818) 279-7788
Fax: (818) 279-5870

Shirts, watches, keychains, etc.

RUBBER STAMPS

The following companies will manufacture rubber stamps to your specifications, including stamps with logos and images made from your artwork. In addition to stamps, most offer a variety of stamp pad colors and other stamp-related supplies. (For more information on rubber stamps, see pages 23-24 in chapter two.)

A STAMP IN THE HAND CO.
20630 S. Leapwood Ave., Ste. B
Carson, CA 90746
(310) 329-8555

BIZARRO
P.O. Box 16160
Rumford, RI 02916
(401) 728-9560

HAMILTON ARTS
5340 Hamilton Ave.
Cleveland, OH 44114
(216) 431-9001

JACKSON MARKING PRODUCTS
Brownsville Road
Mt. Vernon, IL 62864
(800) 851-4945, (618) 242-1334

JAM PAPER & ENVELOPE
111 3rd Ave.
New York, NY 10003
(212) 473-6666
Fax: (212) 473-7300

NAME BRAND
P.O. Box 34245
Potomac, MD 20827
(301) 299-3062
Fax: (301) 299-3063

PRINTING AND FINISHING SERVICES

Chapter

10

ALL KINDS

OF PRINTING

AND OTHER

FINISHING

TECHNIQUES

INK MATCHING SYSTEMS

The following companies offer color mixing and swatch matching systems for printing inks. Each offers its own unique system and accompanying array of swatch books and other color-matching aids. Some offer products that can be purchased off-the-shelf from local art and graphics supply stores.

COLOR CURVE SYSTEMS, INC.
Colwell Industries
200 6th St.
Ft. Wayne, IN 46808
(219) 424-5000
Fax: (219) 424-2710

PANTONE, INC.
55 Knockerbocker Rd.
Moonachi, NJ 07074-9988
(800) 222-1149, (201) 935-5500
Fax: (201) 896-0242

TOYO
Division of Du Pont
2255 Lois Dr.
Rolling Meadows, IL 60048
(800) 277-8696
Fax: (708) 952-0466

ENGRAVERS BY REGION

Engraving is a special process of applying ink to a raised paper surface, providing a distinctive look for letterhead and other applications. The following engravers are all members of the Engraved Stationery Manufacturers Association.

EAST (CT, NH, MA, ME, RI, VT, DC, DE, MD, NJ, NY, PA)

ALL-STATE INTERNATIONAL
1 Commerce Dr.
Cranford, NJ 07016
(800) 222-0510, (908) 272-0800
Fax: (800) 634-5184

ANCHOR ENGRAVING CO., INC.
31-00 47th Ave.
Long Island City, NY 11101
(718) 784-7711
Fax: (718) 784-2683

ARTCRAFT CO., INC.
238 John Dietsch Blvd.
Attleboro Falls, MA 02763
(800) 659-4042, (508) 695-4042
Fax: (508) 699-6769

BATES, JACKSON ENGRAVING CO.
P.O. Box 1128
Buffalo, NY 14205
(716) 854-3000
Fax: (716) 847-1965

CONTINENTAL-BOURNIQUE LTD.
185 Carick St.
New York, NY 10014
(212) 620-0800
Fax: (212) 620-9703

EXCELSIOR-LEGAL, INC.
62 White St.
New York, NY 10013
(800) 221-2972, (212) 431-7000
Fax: (212) 431-5111

EXCELSIOR PROCESS & ENGRAVING
1466 Curran Hwy.
North Adams, MA 01247
(413) 664-4321
Fax: (800) 526-9703

JOHN O. MOONEY CO.
9 Spruce St.
Pawling, NY 12564
(914) 855-4456
Fax: (800) 724-1119

LEHMAN BROTHERS, INC.
191 Foster St.
New Haven, CT 06511
(800) 343-3284, (203) 624-9911
Fax: (203) 624-0374

LS&G IMAGE DYNAMICS
265 W. 40th St.
New York, NY 10018
(212) 302-9059
Fax: (212) 302-9173

P.E. PASCALE & CO.
30-30 Northern Blvd.
Long Island City, NY 11101
(718) 706-1470
Fax: (718) 706-6201

PRECISE CORPORATE PRINTING
75 Front St.
Brooklyn, NY 11201
(800) 392-2496, (718) 243-9000
Fax: (718) 797-9637

VOSE-SWAIN ENGRAVING CO.
411 D. St.
Boston, MA 02210
(617) 542-3711
Fax: (617) 482-4754

SOUTH (AL, FL, GA, KY, LA, MS, NC, SC, TN, TX, VA, WV)

EXCELSIOR-LEGAL, INC.
P.O. Box 2122
Orlando, FL 32802
(800) 327-9220, (407) 299-8220
Fax: (407) 291-6912
Or:
610 Magic Mile Rd.
Arlington, TX 76005
(800) 433-1700, (817) 460-8621
Fax: (817) 461-2677

FINE ARTS ENGRAVING CO.
10490 Marcuson Rd.
Dallas, TX 75238
(214) 553-1500
Fax: (214) 349-5266

H.T. HEARN ENGRAVING CO.
209 Regent Dr.
Winston-Salem, NC 27103
(910) 760-1467
Fax: (910) 760-3370

HARPER ENGRAVING & PRINTING CO.
2318 Mellon Ct.
Decatur, GA 30035
(800) 253-0250, (404) 593-9900
Fax: (404) 593-0974

IVES BUSINESS FORMS, INC.
1009 Camp St.
New Orleans, LA 70130
(504) 561-8811
Fax: (504) 581-4837

SCHMIDT ENGRAVING CO.
1124 Franklin Ave.
Waco, TX 76701
(817) 754-2361
Fax: (817) 753-1139

MIDWEST (IA, IL, IN, MI, MN, MO, OH, WI)

ANDERSON ENGRAVING
311 W. 19th St.
Kansas City, MO 64108
(816) 421-1111
Fax: (816) 842-1649

ARTISTRY ENGRAVING & EMBOSSING CO., INC.
6000 N. Northwest Hwy.
Chicago, IL 60631
(312) 775-4888
Fax: (312) 775-0064

FINE ARTS ENGRAVING CO.
109 Shore Dr.
Burr Ridge, IL 60521
(708) 920-9300
Fax: (708) 920-1524

HARPER ENGRAVING & PRINTING CO.
2626 Fisher Rd.
Columbus, OH 43204
(800) 848-5196, (214) 276-0700
Fax: (214) 276-5557

ROSE ENGRAVING CO.
1435 Fuller, SE
Grand Rapids, MI 49507
(616) 243-3108
Fax: (616) 243-7236

SHIRLEY ENGRAVING CO.
460 Virginia Ave.
Indianapolis, IN 46203
(317) 634-4084
Fax: (317) 685-2524

WEST (CA, CO, KS, NB, ND, NV, SD, UT, WY)

APS ENGRAVERS & LITHOGRAPHERS
120 2nd St.
San Francisco, CA 94105
(415) 392-0979
Fax: (415) 392-0128

If you'd like more information on locating printers, acceptable trade practices and other printing-related issues, contact the trade association, Printing Industries of America, at their national headquarters: 1730 N. Lynn St., Arlington, VA 22209, (703) 841-8100. (There are also a number of local offices in many larger cities.)

BURDGE, INC.
2151 Yates Ave.
Commerce, CA 90040-1900
(213) 722-2011
Fax: (213) 724-7901

THE LIGATURE
3223 E. 46th St.
Los Angeles, CA 90058
(213) 585-2152
Fax: (213) 585-1737

STUART F. COOPER CO.
1565 E. 23rd St.
Los Angeles, CA 90011
(800) 421-8703
Fax: (213) 747-3035

OFFSET LITHOGRAPHERS BY REGION

The following printers have all won recognition for graphic excellence. In addition to setting the standard for excellence in offset printing, they are also known for their ability to capably handle the most challenging printing jobs.

NEW ENGLAND (CT, NH, MA, ME, RI, VT)

ALLIED PRINTING SERVICES, INC.
579 Middle Tpke.
Manchester, CT 06040
(203) 643-1101
Fax: (203) 646-7954

DANIELS PRINTING
40 Commercial St.
Everett, MA 02149
(617) 389-7900
Fax: (617) 389-5520

W.E. ANDREWS CO., INC.
140 South Rd.
Bedford, MA 01720
(617) 275-0720
Fax: (617) 280-3131

MID-ATLANTIC (DC, DE, MD, NJ, NY, PA)

DUNMIRE PRINTING
820 12th St.
Altoona, PA 16602
(814) 944-7733
Fax: (814) 944-3463

L.P. THEBAULT CO.
P.O. Box 169
Parsippany, NJ 07054
(201) 884-1300
Fax: (201) 884-0169

OLD YORK ROAD PRINTING
406 Johnson St.
Abington, PA 19001
(215) 886-3300
Fax: (215) 886-5350

PEAKE PRINTERS, INC.
2500 Schuster Dr.
Chervely, MD 20781
(301) 341-4600
Fax: (301) 341-1162

SOUTHEAST (AL, FL, GA, KY, MS, NC, SC, TN, VA, WV)

CLASSIC GRAPHICS, INC.
P.O. Box 560275
Charlotte, NC 28256-0275
(704) 597-9015
Fax: (704) 597-7041

DICKSON'S
1484 Atlanta Industrial Way
Atlanta, GA 30331
(404) 696-9870

FETTER PRINTING CO.
700 Locust Ln.
Louisville, KY 40213
(502) 634-4771
Fax: (502) 634-3587

GURTNER PRINTING CO.
2033 Cook Dr.
Salem, VA 24153
(703) 772-7835
Fax: (703) 772-7792

JOSTEN'S
2505 Empire Dr.
Winston-Salem, NC 27103
(910) 765-0070
Fax: (910) 659-9423

PROGRESS PRINTING
P.O. Box 4575
Lynchburg, VA 24502
(804) 239-9213
Fax: (804) 237-1618

WASHBURN PRESS
801 S. McDowell St.
Charlotte, NC 28204
(704) 372-5270
Fax: (704) 331-9486

WILLIAMS PRINTING CO.
1240 Spring St., NW
Atlanta, GA 30309
(404) 875-6611
Fax: (404) 872-4025

MIDWEST (IA, IL, IN, MI, MN, MO, OH, WI)

CENTRAL PRINTING CO.
2400 E. River Rd.
Dayton, OH 45439
(513) 298-4321
Fax: (513) 298-6941

DIVERSIFIED GRAPHICS
1700 Broadway
Minneapolis, MN 55413
(612) 331-1111
Fax: (612) 331-4079

THE ETHERIDGE CO.
2450 Oak Industrial Dr.
Grand Rapids, MI 49505
(616) 459-4418
Fax: (616) 459-6043

GREAT NORTHERN/DESIGN PRINTING CO.
5401 Fargo Ave.
Skokie, IL 60077
(312) 775-0220
Fax: (708) 674-4874

H.C. JOHNSON PRESS
P.O. Box 55566
Rockford, IL 61125
(815) 397-0800
Fax: (815) 397-9223

THE HENNEGAN CO.
1001 Plum St.
Cincinnati, OH 45202
(513) 621-7300
Fax: (513) 421-6995

HILLTOP PRESS, INC.
624 E. Walnut St.
Indianapolis, IN 46204
(317) 634-4700
Fax: (317) 634-9682

HM GRAPHICS, INC.
P.O. Box 19901
Milwaukee, WI 53219
(414) 321-6600
Fax: (414) 546-8692

In addition to conventional die-cutting applications such as packaging and pocket folders, HM Graphics also has the capability to print and construct three-dimensional design concepts such as some of the pop-up promotions shown here. See their listing on this page for more information.

If you'd like to know how to best prepare your computer files for press, The Scitex Graphic Arts Users Association publishes a free booklet, the CREF™ Guide *(Computer Ready Electronic Files), a comprehensive guide to electronic prepress techniques. For your copy, contact the Scitex Graphic Arts Users Association at 305 Plus Park Blvd., Nashville, TN 37217; (800) 858-0489, (615) 366-4192; fax: (615) 366-4192.*

JEFFERSON/KEELER
1234 S. Kings Hwy.
St. Louis, MO
(314) 533-8087
Fax: (314) 533-2369

PRINT CRAFT, INC.
315 5th Ave., NW
New Brighton, MN 55112
(612) 633-8122
Fax: (612) 633-1862

SKOKIE VALLEY REPRODUCTIONS
7400 N. Melvina St.
Niles, IL 60648
(708) 647-1131
Fax: (708) 647-2321

UNIQUE PRINTERS AND LITHOGRAPHERS
5500 W. 31st St.
Cicero, IL 60650-3999
(708) 656-8900
Fax: (708) 656-2176

UNIVERSAL LITHOGRAPHERS
3212 Wilgus Rd.
Sheboygan, WI 53081
(414) 452-3401
Fax: (414) 452-2348

WATT/PETERSON, INC.
15020 27th Ave., N.
Plymouth, MN 55947
(612) 553-1617
Fax: (612) 553-0956

SOUTHWEST (AR, AZ, LA, NM, OK, TX)

BUCHANAN PRINTING
2330 Jett St.
Dallas, TX 75234
(214) 241-3311
Fax: (214) 406-6392

HERITAGE PRESS
8939 Premiere Row
Dallas, TX 75245
(214) 637-2700
Fax: (214) 637-2713

IMPERIAL LITHO/GRAPHICS
210 S. 4th Ave.
Phoenix, AZ 85003
(602) 257-8500
Fax: (602) 495-2544

WILLIAMSON PRINTING CORP.
6700 Denton Dr.
Dallas, TX 75235
(214) 352-1122
Fax: (214) 352-1842

WEST (CA, CO, KS, NB, ND, NV, SD, UT, WY)

ANDERSON PRINTING & OFFSET
855 Cahuenga Blvd.
Los Angeles, CA 90038
(213) 460-4115
Fax: (213) 460-6876

COLOR WEST GRAPHICS
2720 Shannon
Santa Ana, CA 92704
(714) 979-9787
Fax: (714) 540-9701

COSTELLO BROTHERS LITHOGRAPHERS
500 S. Palm Ave.
Alhambra, CA 91803-6681
(213) 283-6681
Fax: (213) 283-2094

THE DOT GENERATOR
10621-141 Calle Lee
Los Alamitos, CA 90720
(714) 952-0183
Fax: (714) 952-0870

GEORGE RICE & SONS
2001 N. Soto St.
Los Angeles, CA 90032
(213) 223-2020
Fax: (213) 223-3679

IN TO INK
7888 Silverton Ave., Ste. G
San Diego, CA 92126
(619) 271-6363
Fax: (619) 271-1121

RUSH PRESS
8835 Complex Dr.
San Diego, CA 92123
(619) 292-6906
Fax: (619) 292-1325

SIMON PRINTING
2276 Mora Dr.
Mountain View, CA 94040
(800) 31-SIMON, (415) 965-7170
Fax: (415) 965-7918

NORTHWEST (ID, MT, OR, WA)

HEATH PRINTERS
1617 Boylston Ave.
Seattle, WA 98122
(206) 323-3577
Fax: (206) 323-3577

LETTERPRESS PRINTERS

Letterpress printing offers antique typefaces, a unique debossed finish and a means of printing on handmade, industrial and other unusual papers that offset printers won't touch. The companies listed here not only special- ize in letterpress printing—it's the only kind of print- ing they offer. As a special breed, they not only bring rare expertise to the process, they also offer a high degree of craftsmanship and sensitivity to making the most of the aesthetic potential of this printing method.

CLAUDIA LAUB STUDIO
7404 Beverly Blvd.
Los Angeles, CA 90036
(213) 931-1710
Fax: (213) 931-0126

FIREFLY PRESS
23 Village St.
Sommerville, MA 02143
(617) 625-7500

INDEPENDENT PROJECT PRESS
40 Finley Dr.
P.O. Box 1033
Sedona, AZ 86336
(602) 204-1332
Fax: (602) 204-1332

INNERER KLANG PRESS
7 Sherman St.
Charlestown, MA 02129
(617) 242-0689
Fax: (617) 242-0689

JULIE HOLCOMB PRINTERS
665 3rd St., Ste. 425
San Francisco, CA 94107
(415) 243-0530
Fax: (415) 243-3920

MINDANAO PRINTING
1222 Hazel St., N.
St. Paul, MN 55119-4500
(612) 774-3768
Fax: (612) 771-9772

NADJA
265½ W. 94th St.
New York, NY 10025
(212) 866-5595

PATRICK REAGH PRINTING
1517 Gardena Ave.
Glendale, CA 71204
(818) 241-1805
Fax: (818) 548-2473

PURGATORY PIE PRESS
19 Hudson St., Ste. 403
New York, NY 10013
(212) 274-8228
Fax: (212) 925-3461

QUINTESSENCE WORKING PRESS-ROOM MUSEUM
356 Bunker Hill Mine Rd.
Amador City, CA 95601
(209) 267-5470

RED STAR PRINTING
740 N. Franklin
Chicago, IL 60610
(312) 664-3871
Fax: (312) 664-8961

TIP

Want to know more about letter- press printing? Check out "Letter- pressed Perfec- tion," in *HOW* mag- azine's March/ April, 1991, issue. The article features letterpressed pieces from well-known designers and ad- vice on which pa- pers work best, what typical runs cost and other tech- nical tips.

THE SUN HILL PRESS
12 High St.
North Brookfield, MA 01535
(508) 867-7274
Fax: (508) 867-7274

W. THOMAS TAYLOR
1906 Miriam St.
Austin, TX 78722
(512) 478-7628

WARWICK PRESS
1 Cottage St.
Easthampton, MA 01027
(413) 527-5456

SILKSCREEN PRINTERS

Silkscreen printing offers the opportunity to print on surfaces not possible with a press. You'll find listings for silkscreen printers who specialize in bottles and other packaging applications throughout chapter five. Screen printers that specialize in garments can be found in the Garment Printers section in chapter eight. Others, specializing in label printing, can be found later in this chapter.

This listing includes screen printers offering a range of capabilities and attention to detail that makes them especially qualified to deal with the needs of advertising and graphic designers. They typically handle point-of-purchase, four-color work and are accustomed to meeting tight deadlines. All are members of the SGIA (the Screenprinting & Graphic Imaging Association International), an international association of silkscreen printers.

ABC SIGN AND DISPLAY
341 2nd Ave.
Des Moines, IA 50313
(515) 280-6868
Fax: (515) 280-1066

ADVERTISING DISPLAY CO.
3939 Kearney St.
Denver, CO 80207
(303) 393-9000
Fax: (303) 393-8080

ALBERT BASSE ASSOCIATES
175 Campanelli Pkwy.
Stoughton, MA 02072
(617) 344-3555
Fax: (617) 344-3777

CENTRAL SALES PROMOTIONS, INC.
130 NE 50th St.
Oklahoma City, OK 73152
(404) 525-2335
Fax: (405) 525-3113

CHAMPION SCREEN PRINTING
3901 Virginia Ave.
Cincinnati, OH 45227
(513) 271-3800

DISPLAY CREATIONS, INC.
1970 Industrial Park Rd.
Brooklyn, NY 11207
(718) 257-2300
Fax: (718) 257-2558

DIVERSIFIED SCREEN PRINTING
8B Union Hill Rd.
W. Conshohockan, PA 19428
(610) 828-5444
Fax: (610) 828-7811

FRED B. JOHNSTON CO.
300 E. Boundary Rd.
Chapin, SC 29036
(803) 345-5481
Fax: (803) 345-5512

GANGI STUDIOS, INC.
5265 Vineland Ave.
North Hollywood, CA 91601
(818) 752-4477
Fax: (818) 762-7814

GENERAL SCREEN PRINTING
4520 W. Ohio Ave.
Tampa, FL 33614
(813) 875-0447
Fax: (813) 875-0647

GRADY MCCAULEY, INC.
7584 Whipple Ave.
North Canton, OH 44720
(216) 494-9444
Fax: (216) 494-9991

GRAHAM SCREEN PRINTING
10643 Sentinel Dr.
San Antonio, TX 78217
(210) 654-7641
Fax: (210) 654-7644

GRAPHIC MAGIC
5757 Wilshire Blvd., M101
Los Angeles, CA 90036
(213) 937-5757

IN STORE MEDIA CORP.
510 Wharton Circle
Atlanta, GA 30336
(404) 696-9200
Fax: (404) 691-4522

IVEY-SERIGHT INTERNATIONAL, INC.
427 9th Ave., N.
Seattle, WA 98109
(206) 623-8113
Fax: (206) 467-6297

MILLER-ZELL, INC.
4750 Frederick Dr., SW
Atlanta, GA 30336
(404) 691-7400
Fax: (404) 699-0006

MORRISON & BURKE, INC.
1170 E. Fruit St.
Santa Ana, CA 92701
(714) 547-6511
Fax: (714) 547-0607

PRATT POSTER CO., INC.
3001 E. 30th St.
Indianapolis, IN 46218
(317) 924-3201
Fax: (317) 927-0653

STM GRAPHICS
8401 Chancellor Row
Dallas, TX 75247
(214) 631-6720
Fax: (214) 634-6297

LARGE-SCALE IMAGING AND GRAPHICS

The following companies offer blow-ups of customer-supplied art and transparencies as well as customer-furnished computer files on disk. The process used depends on the company and can include electrostatic, ink-jet, or computerized airbrush. Large-scale imaging is used widely for billboards, vehicle graphics, display and other purposes. Prices vary according to the sub-strate and the type of image. Check with each company to find out which process is most cost-efficient for your needs.

AD GRAPHICS
6601 Lyons Rd., Ste. C-11
Coconut Creek, FL 33073
(800) 645-5740, (305) 421-4669
Fax: (305) 420-5929

Electrostatic printing on adhesive-backed vinyl. Can work from customer-furnished images, including Mac- and PC-compatible files.

ALD DECAL MANUFACTURING
435 Cleveland Ave., NW
Canton, OH 44702
(216) 453-2882
Fax: (216) 453-4313

Offers large-scale imaging on pressure-sensitive decals from translucent Scotchcal™ (for backlit applications) and Scotchlite™ reflective film. Works from customer-furnished art, photos and transparencies.

CACTUS SYSTEMS
P.O. Box 2077
Chino, CA 92708-2077
(909) 628-3265
Fax: (909) 628-0949

Electrostatic and ink-jet printing on adhesive-back, reflective and translucent vinyl as well as paper.

DIGITABLE DIRIGIBLE
417 Canal St.
New York, NY 10013
(212) 431-1925
Fax: (212) 431-1978

Electrostatic printing on paper. Can work with customer-furnished art as well as Mac-compatible computer files.

DIMENSIONAL IMPRESSIONS
4717 Van Nuys Blvd.
Sherman Oaks, CA 91403
(800) 964-7529, (818) 379-7039
Fax: (818) 379-7041

Ink-jet imaging on vinyl, paper foam board and other surfaces. Process suitable for interior usage. Produced from transparencies, Mac- or PC-compatible files.

TIP

If you'd like a list of additional screen printers in your area or want more information on the screen printing industry, contact the SGIA (Screenprinting & Graphic Imaging Association International): 10015 Main St., Fairfax, VA 22031-3489; (703) 385-1335; fax: (703) 359-1336.

GREGORY, INC.
200 S. Regier St.
P.O. Box 410
Buhler, KS 67522
(800) 835-2221, (316) 543-6657
Fax: (800) 835-2221, (316) 543-2690

Scotchprint™ graphics from supplied artwork, including Mac and PC electronic files. Can print on paper, reflective, clear and translucent substrates.

LOWEN COLOR GRAPHICS
1330 E. 4th St.
P.O. Box 1528
Hutchinson, KS 67504-1528
(800) 835-2365, (316) 663-2161
Fax: (316) 663-1429

Utilizes Scotchprint™ technology. Available on opaque, reflective and translucent vinyl films.

MERRITT COLOR IMAGING
650 Franklin Ave.
Hartford, CT 06114
(800) 344-4477, (203) 296-2500
Fax: (203) 296-0414

Scotchprint™ imaging from transparencies, photos or digital files onto adhesive-backed vinyl.

MICHELANGELO SYSTEMS
Belcom Corp.
3135 Madison
Bellwood, IL 60104
(708) 544-4499
Fax: (708) 544-5607

Ink-jet process that can print an image on virtually any substrate, including carpet.

MIRATEC SYSTEMS, INC.
666 Transfer Rd.
St. Paul, MN 55114
(800) 336-1224, (612) 645-8440
Fax: (612) 645-8435

Scotchprint™ imaging from transparencies, photos or digital files.

NSP CORPORATE GRAPHICS
475 N. Daen Rd.
Auburn, AL 36830
(800) 876-6002
Fax: (205) 821-6919

Large-scale graphics on a variety of substrates using the Scotchprint™ electrostatic system.

ONYX GRAPHICS
6915 S. High Tech Dr.
Midvale, UT 84047
(800) 828-0723, (801) 568-9900
Fax: (801) 568-9911

Uses ink-jet process to print on high-gloss paper. Will laminate for increased durability.

REPRO CAD
3650 Mt. Diablo Blvd., Ste. 200
Lafayette, CA 94549
(800) 354-5304, (510) 284-0400
Fax: (510) 283-7864

Mac and PC compatible. Sizes up to forty-two inches wide and 30 feet long. The 800 number refers caller to a nearby service bureau.

SUNGRAF
325 W. Ansin Blvd.
Hallandale, FL 33009
(800) 327-1530, (305) 456-8500
Fax: (305) 454-2266

Digital airbrushed images in sizes up to sixteen feet high and unlimited lengths. Mac and PC compatible.

VISION GRAPHIC TECHNOLOGIES, INC.
2560 W. Directors Row
Salt Lake City, UT 84104
(800) 424-2483, (801) 973-8929
Fax: (801) 973-8944

LAMINATING/DRY MOUNTING

The following companies will laminate and dry mount items for portfolios and other types of presentations, as well as menus, displays, counter cards and more.

ACCENTS & ART
1010 44th Ave.
Oakland, CA 94601
(510) 895-6300
Fax: (510) 895-1420

ACCUPRINT & LAMINATING OF CINCINNATI
49 E. 4th St.
Cincinnati, OH 45202
(513) 651-1078
Fax: (513) 651-5624

CAULASTICS
5955 Mission St.
Daly City, CA 94014
(415) 585-9600
Fax: (415) 585-5209

CENTURY PLUS
2701 Girard NE
Albuquerque, NM 87107
(505) 888-2901
Fax: (505) 888-2902

COMMERCIAL LAMINATING CO.
3131 Chester Ave.
Cleveland, OH 44114
(216) 781-2434
Fax: (216) 781-9413

G2 GRAPHIC SERVICE, INC.
7014 Sunset Blvd.
Los Angeles, CA 90028
(213) 467-7828
(818) 845-8333 (pick-up and delivery)
Fax: (213) 469-0381

INTERNATIONAL LAMINATING
1712 Springfield St.
Dayton, OH 45403
(513) 254-8181
Fax: (513) 256-8813

LAMINATING SERVICES CO.
7359 Varna Ave.
North Hollywood, CA 91605
(818) 982-9065, (213) 460-4104
Fax: (818) 982-2787

PAVLIK LAMINATING
3418 S. 48th St., #8
Phoenix, AZ 85040
(602) 968-4601
Fax: (602) 968-6422

SUPERIOR REPROGRAPHICS
1925 5th Ave.
Seattle, WA 98101
(206) 443-6900
Fax: (206) 441-8390

THERMOGRAPHY

The raised ink surface of thermography is often thought of as an economical way to achieve the impression of engraving. You can order thermographed business cards from most commercial printers or quick print outlets—they will typically farm out your work to a thermographer that specializes in business cards. But if you're looking for more unusual applications of thermography, contact one of these firms.

INK SPOT LITHO
10715 Garvey Ave.
El Monte, CA 91733
(818) 443-1987
Fax: (818) 443-4326

WINSTED
917 SW 10th St.
Hallandale, NJ 33009
(305) 944-7862
Fax: (305) 454-9771

EMBOSSING AND FOIL STAMPING

These companies have a reputation for meeting unusual challenges in foil stamping and embossing.

ARTISTRY ENGRAVING & EMBOSSING CO., INC.
6000 N. Northwest Hwy.
Chicago, IL 60631
(312) 775-4888
Fax: (312) 775-0064

CAPITOL HILL PRINTING
1600 Sherman St.
Denver, CO 80203
(303) 832-2275
Fax: (303) 832-3645

FAUST PRINTING
8656 Utica Ave., #100
Rancho Cucamonga, CA 91730
(909) 980-1577
Fax: (909) 989-9717

GOLDEN STATE EMBOSSING
1251 Folsom St.
San Francisco, CA 94103
(415) 621-2464
Fax: (415) 621-2479

GUNTHER'S PRINTING
16752 Milliken Ave.
Irvine, CA 92714
(714) 833-3500
Fax: (714) 833-3700

KNITTEL ENGRAVING
5195 State Rte. 128
Miamitown, OH 45041
(513) 353-1315
Fax: (513) 353-4300

LABEL, DECAL, NAMEPLATE AND TAPE PRINTERS

The following printers offer a variety of printing techniques, including flexography, letterpress and silkscreen, as well as a wide range of label and decal types, shapes and sizes. In addition to label types mentioned, most also produce bar code labels.

ALL LABEL CORP.
2194 NW 18th Ave.
Miami, FL 33142
(305) 547-2184
Fax: (305) 325-1842

One-color to four-color process printing on acetate, Mylar, paper and foil. Custom die cutting and waterproofing also available.

AMERICAN LABEL
18951 Bonanza Way
Gaithersburg, MD 20879
(800) 438-3568, (301) 670-6170
Fax: (301) 869-2624

Tags, decals and labels. Also prints control panels and name badges. Screen printing on all types of surfaces including Lexan, plastic, vinyl, foil and metal.

AMERICAN NAMEPLATE
4505 S. Kildare Ave.
Chicago, IL 60632
(800) 878-6186, (312) 376-1400
Fax: (312) 376-2236

Custom metal labels and nameplates from aluminum, stainless steel and brass. Also makes labels of mylar, vinyl and aluminum foil.

ANDREWS DECAL CO., INC.
6559 N. Avondale Ave., Dept. N
Chicago, IL 60631-1521
(312) 775-1000
Fax: (312) 775-1001

Offers decals, nameplates, computer labels and pressure-sensitive labels. Flexography, letterpress and silkscreening available. Will print on a variety of materials.

BAY AREA LABELS
1980 Lundy Ave.
San Jose, CA 95131
(800) 229-5223, (408) 432-1980
Fax: (408) 434-6407

Decals and labels from Lexan, polyester, paper and other materials. Offers a variety of print applications, embossing, debossing and holograms. Also makes nameplates and membrane switches.

BAY TECH LABEL, INC.
13161 56th Ct., #204
Clearwater, FL 34620-4027
(800) 229-8321

Prints from one-color to four-color process. Laminating and varnishing also available.

CLASSIC LABELS
130-T New Haven Rd.
Seymour, CT 06483
(203) 881-9855

Custom printed pressure-sensitive labels on rolls, sheets and pinfed. Materials for all applications.

CREATIVE LABELS, INC.
13165 Monterey Rd.
San Martin, CA 95046
(408) 683-0633
Fax: (408) 683-0317

Custom multicolor labels for food, software and more. Also does hang-tags, cards and coupons. Offers short runs with no minimums.

CUMMINS LABEL CO.
2230 Glendening Dr.
Kalamazoo, MI 49003-2042
(616) 345-3386
Fax: (616) 345-6657

Stock and custom-printed labels for many applications, including shipping and packaging. Offers letterpress, flexography and silkscreen printing. No minimum on orders placed.

DELPRINT
2010 S. Carboy
Mt. Prospect, IL 60056
(800) 999-5301, (708) 364-6000

Custom pressure-sensitive labels for packaging and other applications. Also offers in-mold decorating, heat transfers, rub-down products and five types of printing processes.

DESIGN MARK INDUSTRIES
3 Kendrick Rd.
Wareham, MA 02571
(800) 642-7537, (508) 295-9591
Fax: (508) 295-6752

Custom labels, decals and nameplates. Offers one- to four-color process, offset, flexographic and screen printing as well as hot stamping and embossing. District offices in Raleigh, North Carolina, and Philadelphia, Pennsylvania.

EXPRESS CARD AND LABEL CO., INC.
2012 NE Meriden Rd.
Topeka, KS 66608
(800) 862-9408, (913) 233-0369
Fax: (913) 233-2763

Custom labels, tags and coupons in up to eight colors. Multilayer constructions available.

FLEXO TRANSPARENT, INC.
28 Wasson St.
P.O. Box 128
Buffalo, NY 14240
(800) 33-FLEXO, (716) 825-7710
Fax: (716) 825-0139

Manufactures bottle sleeve labels. Stock and custom designs available.

GO TAPE AND LABEL, INC.
19575 NE 10th Ave.
Miami, FL 33179
(800) 468-2731, (305) 652-8300
Fax: (305) 652-8306

Custom labels, tags and tape in all sizes and shapes. Offers one- to four-color process, silkscreening, and hot stamping.

GRAFSTICK TAPE & LABEL
P.O. Box 3277
Framingham, MA 01701
(800) 537-6483
Fax: (508) 620-6229

Custom and preprinted labels in stock.

IDENTIFICATION PRODUCTS CORP.
104 Silliman Ave.
P.O. Box 3276
Bridgeport, CT 06605-0276
(800) 243-9888
Fax: (203) 334-5038

Custom labels on Lexan, foil, vinyl, Mylar and paper. Also makes aluminum nameplates.

INTERMEC MEDIA PRODUCTS
9290 LeSaint Dr.
Fairfield, OH 45014-5454
(800) 881-1303

Bar code labels, tags and ribbons on thermal and thermal transfer papers, plastics and synthetics.

NAMEPLATES FOR INDUSTRY, INC.
213A Rice Blvd.
Industrial Park
New Bedford, MA 02745
(800) 999-8900
Fax: (508) 995-0099

Offers labels, nameplates, decals and tags, screen printed to client specifications. Call for free catalog and samples.

PRECISION TAPE & LABEL, INC.
P.O. Box 374
Millbury, MA 01527-0374
(800) 225-7754, (508) 865-1157
Fax: (508) 865-1161

Custom designed labels in up to six colors.

REED-RITE RELIABLE LABEL CO.
2201 Curtiss St.
Downers Grove, IL 60515
(800) 323-7265, (708) 852-5300
Fax: (708) 852-9604

Decals, pressure-sensitive and static cling labels. Available on rolls and sheets. Offers hot stamping and foil labels.

SCREENPRINT/DOW
271-T Ballardvale St.
P.O. Box 1332
Wilmington, MA 01887
(617) 935-6395
Fax: (508) 658-2307

Nameplates, roll labels and control panels. Offers offset and screen printing, letterpress, hot stamping and flexography.

SETON

P.O. Box DR-1331
New Haven, CT 06505
(800) 243-6624

Custom and stock labels, decals and nameplates on vinyl, polyester, paper, foil and metallic substrates. Call for free catalog and samples.

STAR LABEL

9810 Ashton Rd.
Philadelphia, PA 19114
(800) 394-6900, (215) 677-STAR
Fax: (215) 673-2885, (215) 676-3292

Offers a wide range of labels, decals, tags and nameplates. Printing applications include flexography, letterpress, silkscreening, hot stamping and embossing. Offers up to twelve-color printing.

TECHPRINT

28 6th Rd.
Woburn, MA 01888
(800) 225-2538, (617) 933-8420
Fax: (617) 933-7399

Manufactures custom labels on rolls, strips and as individual pieces. Offset and screen printing, flexography and hot stamping. Also offers nameplates, decals and other items.

ENVELOPE CONVERTERS

When producing envelopes or presentation folders with color or graphics that bleed, these companies will convert preprinted papers and cover stocks into folded and glued final products.

KAROLTON ENVELOPES

511 Byers Rd.
Miamisburg, OH 45402
(800) 235-3660, (513) 859-3661
Fax: (800) 354-0193

LEADER CARDS, INC.

P.O. Box 4607
Milwaukee, WI 53204
(800) 876-2273, (414) 645-5760
Fax: (414) 645-6826

NATIONAL ENVELOPE CORP.

13871 Parks Steed Dr.
Earth City, MO 63045
(314) 291-2722
Fax: (314) 291-1036

NIAGARA ENVELOPE CO.

737 Delaware Ave.
Buffalo, NY 14209
(716) 885-9730
Fax: (716) 885-9746
Or:
14101 E. 33rd Pl.
Aurora, CO 80011
(303) 373-1780
Fax: (303) 371-7765

WILLIAMHOUSE (HEADQUARTERS)

28 W. 23rd St.
New York, NY 10010
(212) 691-2000
Fax: (212) 645-8917

WILLIAMHOUSE

1 Wedding Ln.
Scottdale, PA 15683
(800) 331-4640, (412) 887-5400
Fax: (412) 887-8077
Or:
Vandenburg Dr.
Spence Field Park
Moultrie, GA 31768
(800) 654-5519, (912) 985-7100
Fax: (912) 890-1504
Or:
3800 W. Wisconsin Ave.
Appleton, WI 54915
(800) 558-4808, (414) 733-1014
Fax: (414) 733-4121
Or:
3001 S. Highway 287
Corsicana, TX 75110
(800) 527-2422, (903) 872-5646
Fax: (903) 872-2666
Or:
705 N. Baldwin Park Blvd.
City of Industry, CA 91746
(818) 369-4921
Fax: (818) 369-3532

OTHER

BAY AREA LABELS

1980 Lundy Ave.
San Jose, CA 95131
(800) 229-5223, (408) 432-1980

Makes hologram labels.

IDENTICOLOR
720 White Plains Rd.
Scarsdale, NY 10583
(800) 472-0950, (914) 472-6640
Fax: (914) 472-0954

Specializes in custom rub-down transfers. In addition to standard color rub-downs, company offers foil transfers and hologram transfers.

PINWHEEL
Division of Schaedler Quinzel, Inc.
1279 Rte. 46 E.
Parsippany, NJ 07054
(201) 316-2500
Fax: (212) 684-4543

Specializes in the comping of packaging and other projects requiring short-run screen printing. Also makes custom rub-down transfers.

11 PAPERS

Chapter

DECORATIVE

AND

PRINTING

PAPERS

specialty envelopes

HANDMADE AND SPECIALTY PAPERS

These companies offer handmade, marbled, metallic and otherwise unusual papers that are highly decorative. Most of the handmade papers in this listing aren't offset or laser compatible. Use them for fly leaves, covers, wrappers and applications where letterpress or screen printing will be applied. Check individual listings or call to determine laser and offset compatibility of papers offered.

AIKO'S ART MATERIALS IMPORT
3347 N. Clark St.
Chicago, IL 60657
(312) 404-5600

Offers a large supply of Japanese papers—over two hundred varieties including tie-dyed and stencil-dyed.

AMSTERDAM ART
1013 University Ave.
Berkeley, CA 94710
(800) 994-2787, (510) 649-4800
Fax: (510) 883-0338

Extensive selection of handmade and specialty papers, including Japanese and European handmade papers. Offers the largest collection of Asian papers in the state. Also sells handmade papers from domestic makers.

ATLANTIC PAPERS
P.O. Box 1158
Lemont, PA 16851
(800) 367-8547
Fax: (800) 367-1016

Offers handmade papers from the Czech Republic and Germany suitable for letterheads, invitations and announcements. Also carries matching envelopes. Papers are also available at art supply stores.

DANIEL SMITH
4150 1st Ave. S.
Seattle, WA 98134
(800) 426-6740, (206) 223-9599
Fax: (206) 223-0672

Offers handmade papers from India, Mexico, Japan and Italy, as well as domestic handmade papers. Offers specialty papers, including lace papers, banana paper and genuine papyrus. Also offers other art supplies, such as paints, canvas, brushes, etc. Catalog available.

DIEU DONNE PAPERMILL
433 Broom St.
New York, NY 10013
(212) 226-0573
Fax: (212) 226-6088

New York City-based mill makes and sells its own papers. Specializes in archival rag and custom, handmade papers. Offers a catalog.

THE DIFFRACTION CO.
P.O. Box 151
Riderwood, MD 21139
(410) 666-1144
Fax: (410) 472-4911

Over one hundred patterns of holographic paper in a variety of colors. Comes in rolls or sheets.

EARTH CARE PAPER
966 Mazzoni Rd.
Ukiah, CA 95482-8507
(800) 347-0070
Fax: (707) 468-9486

Sells papers in small quantities from "environmentally responsible" mills. Offers a catalog.

ELICA'S
1801 4th St.
Berkeley, CA 94710
(510) 845-9530
Fax: (510) 845-5619

Offers over two hundred varieties of Japanese papers including stencil-dyed and tie-dyed papers. Offers a free catalog.

EVANESCENT PRESS
P.O. Box 64
Leggett, CA 95585
(707) 925-6494
Fax: (707) 925-6472

Offers domestic handmade papers. Also does letterpress printing and hand book binding, and distributes hemp fiber and other natural materials. Offers a price list and sample swatches.

FLAX ART & DESIGN
Collage (catalog)
P.O. Box 7216
San Francisco, CA 94120-7216
(415) 468-7530

Stocks hundreds of types of handmade and hand-decorated papers, both domestic and imported. Offers two free catalogs.

FLAX ART MATERIALS
62 E. Randolph
Chicago, IL 60601
(312) 580-2535
Fax: (312) 263-3738

Offers Japanese handmade papers and Wyndstone™ papers.

JAM PAPER & ENVELOPE
111 3rd Ave.
New York, NY 10003
(212) 473-6666
Fax: (212) 473-7300

Offers a free catalog.

THE JAPANESE PAPER PLACE
887 Queen W.
Toronto, Ontario M6J 1G5
Canada
(416) 703-0089
Fax: (416) 703-0163

Carries over two hundred handmade Japanese papers and provides a sample service. Cash and carry is preferred. Minimum ship order is $50.

KATE'S PAPERIE
8 W. 13th St.
New York, NY 10011
(212) 633-0570
Fax: (212) 366-6532

New York City-based outlet carries a variety of handmade papers and offers a sample service. Also sells paper-making supplies, instructional materials and kits.

LOOSE ENDS
P.O. Box 20310
Keizer, OR 97307
(503) 390-7457
Fax: (503) 390-4724

Specializes in paper products with a natural, kraft look and heavily textured handmade papers. Also stocks kraft bags, corrugated paper and boxes, natural gift wrap, raffia and other nature-inspired products. Offers a free catalog.

MAGNOLIA EDITIONS
2527 Magnolia St.
Oakland, CA 94607
(510) 839-5268
Fax: (510) 893-8334

Makes and sells custom papers. Papers are suitable for letterpress or screen printing but are not offset compatible. Will sell overstock of its custom papers.

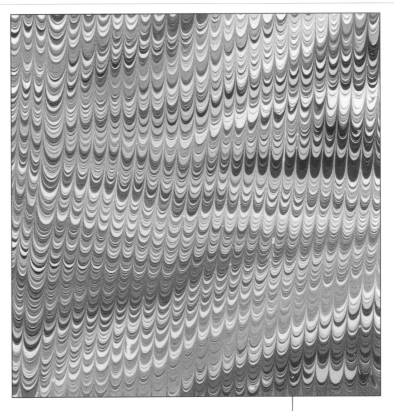

NEW YORK CENTRAL ART SUPPLY
62 3rd Ave.
New York, NY 10003
(800) 950-6111, (212) 473-7705
Fax: (212) 475-2542 (store)
(212) 475-2513 (warehouse)

Approximately twenty-five hundred kinds of paper in stock from all over the world. Handmade and hand-marbled papers a specialty. Catalog available.

THE PAPER SOURCE
232 W. Chicago Ave.
Chicago, IL 60610
(312) 337-0798
Fax: (312) 337-0798

Oriental, handmade, commercial and specialty papers. Also offers classes on book making, box making, etc.

SEMPER PAPER
40-14 24th St.
Long Island City, NY 11001
(718) 383-2826

Offers pearlescent, moiré patterned, foil-textured and other unusual papers, many suitable for offset printing.

New York Central Art Supply carries many types of handmade and hand-marbled papers such as this hand-marbled paper by Iris Nevins. For more information, see Central's listing at left.

If you're looking for industrial papers such as kraft or corrugated cardboard, chipboard, packing or butcher paper, check out your local paper converter or distributor. They can usually be found in your local yellow pages or business-to-business directory. Art supply stores are also a good source for small quantities of newsprint paper.

TWIN ROCKER PAPER MILL
100 E. 3rd St.
P.O. Box 413
Brookston, IN 47923
(317) 563-3119

Mill makes its own papers in sizes up to 4′×8′. Also makes custom papers and specializes in small quantities. Takes mail orders and also sells many of its papers through art supply stores.

VAN LEER METALLIZED PRODUCTS
24 Forge Pk.
Franklin, MA 02038
(800) 343-6977, (508) 541-7700
Fax: (508) 541-7777

Carries holographic papers in a variety of colors and patterns. Offers a sample kit of their products.

VICKI SCHOBER CO.
2363 N. Mayfair Rd.
Milwaukee, WI 53226
(414) 476-8000
Fax: (414) 476-8041

Milwaukee-based paper supply firm. Offers over six hundred types of papers including marbled and other decorative types such as bark, lace and rice papers.

WYNDSTONE
Graphic Arts Products Corp.
1480 S. Wolf Rd.
Wheeling, IL 60090-6514
(708) 537-9300

Manufactures specialty papers with distinctive textures and finishes. Available at most art supply stores, Wyndstone also sells a specifier with 186 sample swatches of its papers for $39.95.

PAPER-MAKING SUPPLIES AND INSTRUCTIONAL MATERIALS

If you want to make your own paper, these companies can show you how and supply you with the equipment you need.

DIEU DONNE PAPERMILL
433 Broom St.
New York, NY 10013
(212) 226-0573
Fax: (212) 226-6088

GOLD'S ARTWORKS INC.
2100 N. Pine St.
Lumberton, NC 28358
(800) 356-2306, (919) 739-9605

KATE'S PAPERIE
8 W. 13th St.
New York, NY 10011
(212) 633-0570
Fax: (212) 366-6532

MAGNOLIA EDITIONS
2527 Magnolia St.
Oakland, CA 94607
(510) 839-5268
Fax: (510) 893-8334

TWIN ROCKER PAPER MILL
100 E. 3rd St.
P.O. Box 413
Brookston, IN 47923
(317) 563-3119

LASER-COMPATIBLE SPECIALTY PAPERS

These companies offer papers that can be run through laser printers or photocopiers. In addition to simulating parchment, coated and flocked papers, and many other commercial printing papers that may not be laser-compatible, most of these manufacturers sell papers that have been preprinted with backgrounds, borders and other graphics. You'll also find laser-compatible labels, Rolodex™ cards, certificates and other items that go beyond ordinary papers. All of the companies in this listing will take mail orders. Call them for a free catalog or sample pack.

IDEA ART
P.O. Box 291505
Nashville, TN 37229-1505
(800) 433-2278
Fax: (800) 435-2278

Offers over one thousand preprinted designs on laser-compatible paper for letterhead, newsletters, cards, invitations, tri-fold brochures and certificates.

PAPARAZZI PAPERS

Letraset USA
40 Eisenhower Dr.
Paramus, NJ 07653
(800) 526-9073
Fax: (201) 845-5047

Preprinted papers and coordinated envelopes with gradated color blends, simulated textures, borders and other graphic effects. Some designs include coordinated business cards. Available at most art supply stores.

PAPER ACCESS

23 W. 18th St.
New York, NY 10011
(800) PAPER-01, (212) 463-7035
Fax: (212) 463-7022

Offers over two hundred paper products including papers preprinted with borders and textures, laser-compatible mill papers in small quantities and specialty papers such as crack-and-peel labels. New York address serves as a retail outlet.

PAPER DESIGN WAREHOUSE

1720 Oak St.
Lakewood, NJ 08701
(800) 836-5400
Fax: (908) 367-3672

Mail order house for the laser-compatible specialty papers in this section. Also stocks transparency film for overhead projector presentations, as well as laminating and plastic comb and strip binding systems.

PAPERDIRECT

100 Plaza Dr.
Secaucus, NJ 07094-3606
(800) A-PAPERS
Fax: (201) 271-9601

Papers preprinted with patterns and borders including coordinated packages consisting of three-panel mailers, postcards, business cards, presentation folders, envelopes and more. Also offers unprinted papers, envelopes and labels.

QUEBLO IMAGES

1000 Florida Ave.
Hagerstown, MD 21741
(800) 523-9080
Fax: (800) 55-HURRY

Offers scored and perforated papers that include business reply cards, tent cards with unusual shapes, preprinted papers and unusual papers such as woodchip and parchment. Also offers envelope labels, foil holiday cards and books.

Love the look of industrial stock but need a paper that's laser-compatible? French Paper carries a line of printing papers under the name Dur-O-Tone™ that includes construction, newsprint, butcher, packing and kraft paper. All of them are offset compatible, and the butcher paper and newsprint lines are also laser-compatible. Contact your local French Paper merchant or contact French Paper directly to locate a merchant in your area—the company's address and phone number are listed on page 113.

WILLIAMHOUSE

28 W. 23rd St.
New York, NY 10010
(212) 691-2000
Fax: (212) 645-8917

Stocks presentation folders with matching envelopes, laser-compatible announcement papers with recessed panels and foil edges, plus other types of papers.

SMALL QUANTITIES OF SPECIALTY ENVELOPES

These companies sell blank envelopes ranging from invitation-sized to folder-sized. Many types of envelopes can also be found at the retail outlets that sell small quantities of mill papers listed elsewhere in this chapter. For manila envelopes and preprinted business envelopes, check listings for office supplies on page 6 in chapter one. For custom envelopes see Envelope Converters in chapter ten.

JAM PAPER & ENVELOPE

111 3rd Ave.
New York, NY 10003
(800) 8010-JAM, (212) 473-7300
Fax: (212) 473-7300

In addition to all types and colors of envelopes including foil-lined, the company sells a variety of presentation folders with matching booklet envelopes. Call for a free catalog.

WILLIAMHOUSE

28 W. 23rd St.
New York, NY 10010
(212) 691-2000
Fax: (212) 645-8917

This envelope converter will also sell small quantities of its stock envelopes in a variety of sizes and colors.

SOURCES FOR FINE PRINTING PAPERS— MAJOR MANUFACTURERS

Contact the following paper manufacturers for swatch books of their printing papers. Many of these mills also offer technical guide books and promotional brochures that demonstrate how their papers perform under various printing and finishing techniques. Some will also utilize their papers to make up comps of folders, boxes, brochures and other items, custom-made to your specifications. When calling, ask for the sample department or customer service.

TIP

Looking for information on recycled papers? The AIGA offers a book, *Recycled Papers: The Essential Guide*, that explains what to look for when specifying a recycled paper. The book retails for $27.06. Contact the AIGA at 1059 3rd Ave., New York, NY 10021; (212) 807-1990; Fax: (212) 807-1799.

APPLETON PAPERS, INC.
825 E. Wisconsin Ave.
P.O. Box 359
Appleton, WI 54912
(800) 922-1725, (414) 734-9841
Fax: (414) 749-8796

ARJO WIGGINS
600 W. Puttman Ave.
Greenwich, CT 06830
(203) 622-4503
Fax: (203) 622-4550

BECKETT PAPER CO.
400 Dayton St.
Hamilton, OH 45012
(800) 543-1188, (513) 863-5641
Fax: (513) 896-2535

Also offers custom papers matched to your color and flocking specifications.

CHAMPION INTERNATIONAL CORP.
1 Champion Plaza
Stamford, CT 06921
(203) 358-7000

CONSERVATREE
10 Lombard St., Ste. 350
San Francisco, CA 94111
(415) 433-1000

CONSOLIDATED PAPERS, INC.
181 W. Madison St.
Chicago, IL 60602
(312) 781-0200
Fax: (312) 781-0259

CRANE & CO. INC.
30 South St.
Dalton, MA 01226
(413) 684-2600
Fax: (413) 684-4278

CROSS POINTE PAPER CORP.
1295 Bandana Blvd. N., Ste. 335
St. Paul, MN 55108
(612) 644-3644
Fax: (612) 644-3981

DECORATED PAPER CORP.
8th and Erie Sts.
Camden, NJ 08102
(609) 365-4200
Fax: (609) 365-0102

DOMTAR
P.O. Box 7211
Montreal, Quebec H3C 3M2
Canada
(800) 267-3060, (514) 848-5400
Fax: (800) 267-8899

E.B. EDDY FOREST PRODUCTS LTD.
1600 Scott St.
Ottawa, Ontario K1Y 4N7
Canada
(800) 267-0702, (613) 782-2600
Fax: (613) 725-6759

EASTERN FINE PAPER, INC.
P.O. Box 129
Brewer, ME 04412
(207) 989-7070
Fax: (207) 989-4663

FINCH PRUYN CO., INC.
1 Glen St.
Glen Falls, NY 12801
(518) 793-2541
Fax: (518) 743-9656

FLETCHER PAPER CO.
318 W. Fletcher
Alpena, MI 49707
(800) 634-3158, (517) 354-2131
Fax: (517) 356-5288

FOX RIVER PAPER CO.
200 E. Washington St.
Appleton, WI 54913
(414) 733-7341
Fax: (414) 733-2975

Also offers custom papers matched to your color and flocking specifications. Will make papers with custom watermarks. (For minimum quantities, call or ask your local paper merchant.)

FRENCH PAPER CORP.
P.O. Box 398
Niles, MI 49120
(616) 683-1100
Fax: (616) 683-3025

Offers custom papers matched to your color and flocking specifications.

GEORGE WHITING
P.O. Box 28
Menasha, WI 54952
(414) 722-3351
Fax: (414) 722-9553

GILBERT PAPER
Division of Mead
430 Ahnaip St.
Menasha, WI 54952
(800) 992-2311, (414) 722-7721
Fax: (800) 445-6309

Offers custom papers matched to your color and flocking specifications. Will make papers with custom watermarks. (For minimum quantities, call or ask your local paper merchant.)

HAMMERMILL PAPERS
6400 Poplar Ave.
Memphis, TN 38197
(800) 633-6369, (901) 763-7800
Fax: (901) 763-6396

HOPPER PAPER CO.
A Division of Georgia Pacific
P.O. Box 105237
Atlanta, GA 30348
(800) 727-3738, (404) 521-4000
Fax: (800) 283-7460

HOWARD PAPER
Division of Fox Paper
P.O. Box 982
Dayton, OH 54401-0982
(800) 558-8327, (513) 427-4077
Fax: (800) 257-6508

ISLAND PAPER MILLS
P.O. Box 2170
New Westminster, B.C. V3L 5A5
Canada
(800) 663-6221, (604) 527-2610
Fax: (604) 526-0701

JAMES RIVER CORP.
300 Lakeside Dr., 14th Fl.
Oakland, CA 94612
(800) 441-9292, (510) 452-3100
Fax: (510) 896-4505

Offers custom papers matched to your color and flocking specifications.

LYONS FALLS PULP & PAPER
Center St.
P.O. Box 338
Lyons Falls, NY 13368
(800) 648-4458, (315) 348-8629
Fax: (315) 348-8629

MEAD CORP.
Fine Paper Division
Courthouse Plaza NE
Dayton, OH 45463
(800) 638-3313, (513) 222-6323
Fax: (513) 495-3192

MOHAWK PAPER MILLS, INC.
465 S. Saratoga St.
P.O. Box 497
Cohoes, NY 12047
(800) THE-MILL, (518) 237-1740
Fax: (518) 233-7102

Offers custom papers matched to your color and flocking specifications.

MONADNOCK PAPER MILLS, INC.
117 Antrim Rd.
Bennington, NH 03442-4205
(603) 588-3311
Fax: (603) 588-3158

NEENAH PAPER
Division of Kimberly Clark Corp.
1376 Kimberly Dr.
Neenah, WI 54956
(800) 338-6077, (414) 587-8000
Fax: (414) 721-3833

PARSONS
2270 Beaver Rd.
Landover, MD 20785
(301) 386-4700
Fax: (301) 773-7864

PENNTECH PAPERS, INC.
181 Harbor Dr.
Stamford, CT 06902
(800) 458-4640, (203) 356-1850
Fax: (203) 324-3782

PERMALIN PRODUCTS CO.
109 W. 26th St.
New York, NY 10001
(800) 544-3454, (212) 627-7750
Fax: (212) 463-9812

POTLATCH CORP.
100 Pringle Ave., Ste. 400
Walnut Creek, CA 94596-6192
(800) 227-4435, (510) 947-4700
Fax: (510) 947-4793

REPAP SALES CORP.
301 Tresser Blvd.
Stamford, CT 06901-3235
(203) 353-3333
Fax: (203) 353-5805

ROOSEVELT PAPER CO.
7601 State Rd.
Philadelphia, PA 19136-3496
(800) 523-3470, (215) 331-5000
Fax: (215) 338-1199

S.D. WARREN CO.
Division of Scott Paper
225 Franklin St.
Boston, MA 02110
(800) 882-4332, (617) 423-7300
Fax: (617) 423-5491

SEMPER PAPER
40-14 24th St.
Long Island City, NY 11001
(718) 383-2826
Fax: (718) 786-5603

SIMPSON PAPER CO.
1301 5th Ave.
Seattle, WA 98101
(206) 224-5700
Fax: (206) 224-5899

SPRINGHILL PAPER
Division of International Paper Co.
2 Manhattanville Rd.
Purchase, NY 10577
(914) 397-1500
(800) 223-1268

STRATHMORE PAPER CO.
39 S. Broad St.
Westfield, MA 01085
(800) 628-8816, (413) 568-9111
Fax: (800) 331-9167

TIP

If your project is printed on recycled paper and you want people to know, get the official "Printed on Recycled Paper" icon from the American Forest and Paper Association. Contact them at 1111 19th St., NW, Ste. 800, Washington, DC 20036; (202) 463-2700; Fax: (202) 463-2783.

Offers custom papers matched to your color and flocking specifications.

UK PAPER NORTH AMERICA
Division of Consort Royal Papers
500 State Rd.
Bensalem, PA 19020
(800) 220-UKPS
Fax: (215) 639-2005

WESTVACO CORP.
Fine Papers Division
399 Park Ave.
New York, NY 10171
(212) 688-5000
Fax: (212) 318-5075

WEYERHAUSER PAPER CO.
P.O. Box 829
Valley Forge, PA 19382
(610) 251-9220
Fax: (610) 647-2002

ZANDERS USA
100 Demarest Dr.
Wayne, NJ 07470
(201) 305-1990
Fax: (201) 305-1888

SOURCES OF SMALL QUANTITIES OF MILL PAPERS

If you'd like to purchase a ream or less of the printing papers produced by the paper manufacturers listed in this chapter, these outlets sell these papers and matching envelopes in small quantities off the shelf.

ARVEY
3352 W. Addison
Chicago, IL 60618
(800) 866-6332, (312) 463-6423

Forty locations in major U.S. cities. Call the number above for the nearest location.

IF IT'S PAPER
3900 Spring Garden St.
Greensboro, NC 27407
(910) 299-1211

A division of Dillard Paper Co., this retail division includes over forty-one stores in North Carolina,

South Carolina, Virginia, Georgia, Tennessee and Alabama.

KELLY PAPER
1441 E. 16th St.
Los Angeles, CA 90021
(800) 67-KELLY, (213) 749-1311

Twenty-two locations in California, Arizona and Nevada.

LIMITED PAPERS
80 Washington St.
New York, NY 10006
(212) 797-7022

Takes mail orders. Call for free catalog.

PAPER ACCESS
23 W. 18th St.
New York, NY 10011
(800) PAPER-01, (212) 463-7035

Will handle mail orders. Call for free catalog.

PAPER AND GRAPHIC SUPPLY CENTERS
200 Howard St.
Detroit, MI 48216
(800) 477-0050, (313) 496-3131

Affiliated with Seaman-Patrick. Offers retail centers in eleven cities throughout Michigan and Ohio.

THE PAPER SHOP
2385 Maryland Rd.
Willow Grove, PA 19090
(215) 657-7630

Over seventeen locations in the Northeast.

PARSONS
2270 Beaver Rd.
Landover, MD 20785
(301) 386-4700

Will take phone orders for its papers.

PRESS STOCK/THE SUPPLY ROOM
3131 New Mark Dr.
Miamisburg, OH 45342
(800) 822-6323, (513) 495-6000

A division of Zellerbach, this retail division has over thirty-one stores in major metropolitan areas.

INTERACTIVE MULTIMEDIA

Chapter 12

SERVICES, EQUIPMENT AND

OTHER RESOURCES FOR

INTERACTIVE KIOSKS,

CD-ROMS AND

MULTIMEDIA

PRESENTATIONS

STOCK CLIPS

These companies offer video and still images and audio for multimedia productions for a users fee.

FILM AND VIDEO FOOTAGE

A.R.I.Q. FOOTAGE
3 Goodfriend Dr.
East Hampton, NY 11937
(800) 249-1940, (516) 329-9200
Fax: (516) 329-9260

Historical and musical-performance library consists of fifteen thousand hours of footage from 1896 to 1980. Available on film.

ACTION SPORTS ADVENTURE
1926 Broadway, 5th Fl.
New York, NY 10023
(212) 721-2800
Fax: (212) 721-0191

Collection includes more than twelve thousand hours of 16mm and 35mm material, including Olympic and historic sports footage from the 1950s to the present. Available on film and video.

AERIAL FOCUS
8 Camino Verde
Santa Barbara, CA 93103
(805) 962-9911
Fax: (805) 962-9536

Subject matter focuses on adventure sports such as skydiving and hang gliding. Also offers aerial footage of the earth. Available on film and video.

DIGITAL ANIMATION CORP.
24445 Northwestern Hwy., Ste. 105
Southfield, MI 48075
(800) 572-0098, (810) 354-0890
Fax: (810) 354-0796

Offers 3-D animation packages designed for video broadcast producers. Also offers copyright-free still images. Available on video and QuickTime.

FABULOUS FOOTAGE
1680 N. Vine St., Ste. 1017
Hollywood, CA 90028
(800) 665-5368, (213) 463-1153
Fax: (213) 463-1391
Or:
19 Mercer St.
Toronto, Ontario M5Z 1H2
Canada
(800) 361-3456, (416) 591-6955
Fax: (416) 591-1666

Also has locations in Boston (same 800 number as for the Toronto location) and Vancouver (same 800 number as for the California location). Subjects include international, business, sports, wildlife and archival clips. Also carries slapstick comedy and sports bloopers. Available on film, video and CD-ROM.

FOUR PALMS ROYALTY FREE DIGITAL VIDEO
11260 Roger Bacon Dr.
Reston, VA 22090
(800) 7-4PALMS, (703) 759-7200
Fax: (703) 759-9473

Offers hundreds of video sequences of scenery, sports, transportation and lifestyle images. Subjects are professionally shot and compressed to AVI format. Video collections on CD-ROM start at $99 per disc.

HARDY JONES PRODUCTIONS
1252 B St.
Petaluma, CA 94952
(707) 769-0708
Fax: (707) 769-0708

Specializes in ocean-related footage such as fish, sea birds and marine mammals. Available on film, video and QuickTime.

INTERNATIONAL HISTORIC FILMS
3533 S. Archer Ave.
Chicago, IL 60609
(312) 927-2900
Fax: (312) 927-9211

Offers military and political subject matter dating back to the turn of the century. Collection includes rare newsreels and propaganda films from Germany and the Soviet Union. Available on video. Also offers photographic stills.

MEDIA-PEDIA
22 Fisher Ave.
Wellesley, MA 02181
(617) 237-3440

Offers buy-out collection of current and historical images covering nature, technology and people. Fifty-minute video collection costs $249 to $495, depending on format. Available on CD-ROM and video.

MIRAMAR PRODUCTIONS
200 2nd Ave., W.
Seattle, WA 98119
(800) 245-6472, (206) 284-4700
Fax: (206) 286-8043

Specializes in nature and computer-generated imagery. Includes time-lapse and aerial-view clips. Available on film, laserdisc and video.

NATIONAL GEOGRAPHIC FILM LIBRARY
810 7th Ave.
New York, NY 10019
(212) 841-4460
Fax: (212) 944-4856
Or:
1145 17th St., NW
Washington, DC 20036
(202) 857-7659
Fax: (202) 429-5755
Or:
4370 Tujunga Ave., Ste. 300
Studio City, CA 91604
(818) 506-8300
Fax: (818) 506-8200

Three locations. Extensive library contains close to ten million feet of film on nature, adventure and wildlife. Available in many kinds of video formats.

MULTIMEDIA CLIP ART

Multimedia images don't require the high resolution necessary for print applications (three hundred dpi or more). Because standard screen resolution of seventy-two dpi is all that's necessary, many of the low-res clip art images offered in the listings in the illustration and photography chapters can be used in multimedia applications as still images. The clip libraries listed here were developed with the special needs of multimedia in mind and can be animated or be incorporated into user interface designs.

CLASSIC TEXTURES
% Pixar
1001 W. Cutting Blvd.
Richmond, CA 94804
(800) 888-9856, (510) 236-4000

Offers a library of photographic textures such as fur, water and marble on CD-ROM. Can be used with any application that reads PICT or TIFF files on Mac, PC and UNIX computers. Collections start at $99 per disc.

DIGITAL ANIMATION CORP.
24445 Northwestern Hwy., Ste. 105
Southfield, MI 48075
(800) 572-0098, (810) 354-0890
Fax: (810) 354-0796

Offers collections of backgrounds; globes, maps and flags; holidays; advertising; broadcast and corporate-related images. Also offers 3-D animation packages designed for video broadcast producers.

IMAGETECTS
7200 Bollinger Rd., Ste. 2
San Jose, CA 95129
(408) 252-5487
Fax: (408) 252-7409

Collection includes 1,150 textures, backgrounds and objects. Mac-, PC-, Amiga- and UNIX-compatible images available on CD-ROM.

LETRASET USA
40 Eisenhower Dr.
Paramus, NJ 07653
(800) 526-9073
Fax: (201) 845-5047

CD-ROM collection of background subjects consists of 360 versatile images including leaves, rocks and other nature-related subjects, industrial images and sports activities.

STUDIO PRODUCTIONS
18000 E. 400 S.
Elizabethtown, IN 47232
(800) 359-2964, (513) 251-7014
Fax: (513) 861-2932

Collection on CD-ROM consists of templates for multimedia interface design. Includes "floating" panels, three-dimensional buttons, title pages and background effects.

CLIP AUDIO

These companies offer royalty-free music and sound effects that can be used in multimedia presentations.

CAMBIUM DEVELOPMENT, INC.
P.O. Box 296-H
Scarsdale, NY 10583
(800) 231-1779, (914) 472-6246
Fax: (914) 472-6729

CHAMELEON MUSIC
2A Mansion Woods Dr.
Agawam, MA 01001
(800) 789-8779

CREATIVE SUPPORT SERVICES
1948 Riverside Dr.
Los Angeles, CA 90039
(800) HOT-MUSIC, (213) 666-7968

THE MUSIC BAKERY
7522 Campbell Rd.
Dallas, TX 75248
(800) 229-0313

TIP

For additional multimedia resources, check out the *Multimedia Source Book*, an industry guide featuring over six thousand listings of related manufacturers, services and talent. It can be purchased for $49.95 from Multimedia, 445 5th Ave., Ste. 27H, New York, NY 10016; (800) 696-9646, (212) 293-3900.

One of the best places to locate multimedia talent is on the World Wide Web where freelancers and other multimedia specialists advertise their services. If you don't have access to the Web, another source for multimedia talent is New Media Showcase, a directory devoted to multimedia and animation freelancers that contains over three hundred images representing these artists. Contact New Media at: 915 Broadway, 14th Fl., New York, NY 10010; (800) 894-7469, (212) 673-6600; fax: (212) 673-9795.

INDUSTRY ORGANIZATIONS

ACM/SIGGRAPH

401 N. Michigan Ave.
Chicago, IL 60611
(312) 321-6830
Fax: (312) 321-6876

First formed in 1973 as the Association for Computing Machinery, this international organization now consists of eighty thousand members. The group offers a variety of publications and local chapter workshops, as well as the annual SIGGRAPH conference and exhibition. (For more information on SIGGRAPH, see the listing in this chapter under Trade Shows, pages 120-121.)

ICIA

(International Communications
Industries Association)
3150 Spring St.
Fairfax, VA 22031
(703) 273-7200
Fax: (703) 278-8082

The International Communications Industries Association sponsors an annual conference and trade show, INFOCOMM International. Organization also publishes a monthly tabloid and a membership directory.

NATIONAL MULTIMEDIA ASSOCIATION OF AMERICA

4920 Niagara Rd., Ste. 307
College Park, MD 20740
(800) 214-9531, (301) 474-4107

Formed in 1993, this group is now ten thousand strong. Offers a monthly magazine, seminars and trade shows, and a national job bank on the Internet. Also offers shareware and software discounts.

TRADE SHOWS

Some of the best opportunities for learning about the latest developments in interactive multimedia are trade shows and conferences featuring state-of-the-art technologies.

ELECTRONIC IMAGING: SCIENCE & TECHNOLOGY

IS&T/SPIE (Society for Imaging
Science & Technology)
7003 Kilworth Ln.
Springfield, VA 22151
(703) 642-9090

Exhibition and conference featuring the latest developments in digital imaging and multimedia. Sponsored by the IS&T/SPIE, the location of this annual conference changes from year to year.

INFOCOMM INTERNATIONAL

(International Communication
Industries Association)
3150 Spring St.
Fairfax, VA 22031
(800) 345-EXPO, (703) 273-7200
Fax: (703) 278-8082

Annual trade show features conferences and expositions that focus on the latest developments in video and multimedia technology.

INTERMEDIA

Reed Exhibition Companies
383 Main Ave.
Norwalk, CT 06851
(203) 840-5634
Fax: (203) 840-9634

Annual conference and exhibition features lectures from industry leaders and educational workshops. Location varies from year to year. (To be held in San Francisco in March, 1996.)

MACWORLD EXPO

Mitch Hall Associates
260 Milton St.
Dedham, MA 02026
(617) 361-2001
Fax: (617) 361-5923

Two shows held annually: one in Boston and one in San Francisco. Features the latest hardware and software developments for a Macintosh platform. Includes print as well as multimedia technologies.

MULTIMEDIA EXPOSITION AND FORUM
Plum Studios
7-70 Villarboit Crescent
Concord, Ontario L4K 4C7
Canada
(905) 660-2491
Fax: (905) 660-2492

Canadian conference and trade show featuring over sixty-five seminars and workshops by industry experts.

SEYBOLD SEMINARS AND DIGITAL WORLD
% Softbank Exposition and Conference Co.
303 Vintage Park Dr., Ste. 201
Foster City, CA 94404-1138
(800) 433-5200, (415) 578-6900
Fax: (415) 525-0199

Softbank Exposition and Conference Co. sponsors a number of conference/exposition events each year. Of particular interest are the Seybold Seminars (one held in Boston each spring and one in San Francisco each fall). Seybold Seminars feature computer graphics and publishing. Digital World, held in Los Angeles each summer, features digital imaging and multimedia, with an emphasis on the entertainment industry.

SIGGRAPH
401 N. Michigan Ave.
Chicago, IL 60611
(312) 321-6830
Fax: (312) 321-6876

Annual conference and exhibition is one of the largest in the U.S., offering the latest in computer graphics and interactive techniques as well as the newest developments in cyberspace, entertainment media, interactive digital techniques and more. Usually held in later summer, location changes every year.

VIDEO EXPO
Knowledge Industries Publications
701 Westchester Ave.
White Plains, NY 10604
(800) 800-5474, (914) 328-9156

Annual trade show and exhibition at the Jacob K. Javits Convention Center in New York City. Features seminars, workshops and over two hundred exhibits of video, multimedia, graphics and animation hardware and software.

Using interactive (electronic) magazines is a great way to update yourself on the latest trends in multimedia. For starters, check out NautilusCD— released in 1990, this was one of the first magazines launched on CD-ROM, and features program demos, copyright-free samples of photos, shareware, music, video and games. Contact NautilusCD, Metatec, 7001 Metatec Blvd., Dublin, OH 43017; (800) 637-3472, (614) 761-2000. Another good bet is Fuse, the brainchild of renowned designer Neville Brody. Fuse, out of London, is available on the Internet and through FontShop USA at (800) 363-6687.

SERVICES AND EQUIPMENT

CATALOGIC
2685 Marine Way
Mountain View, CA 94043
(415) 961-4649
Fax: (800) 255-4020, (415) 964-2027

Manufacturer of CD-ROM discs. Can create masters and duplications. Handles insert printing and packaging. Advertises one thousand CDs for $2,000. Offers a catalog on the Internet. Internet address: sales@catalogic.com.

PIXEL TOUCH
1914 Bon View Ave., Ste. 11
Ontario, CA 91761
(800) 39-TOUCH, (909) 923-6124

Manufactures touch screen monitors, televisions and touch pads.

PRODUCTS INTERACTIVE, INC.
1555 Oakbrook Dr., Ste. 145
Norcross, GA 30093
(800) 891-9344, (404) 448-9599
Fax: (404) 448-0121

Manufactures touch-screen monitors for interactive kiosks used for point-of-purchase displays, public information systems and for interactive training. ·

ONLINE SERVICES

These online services have a lot to offer for graphic designers and other graphic arts professionals, including services for multimedia designers.

AMERICA ONLINE
8619 Westwood Center Dr.
Vienna, VA 22182-2285
(800) 827-6364, (703) 448-8700

Access through e-mail to other design firms, design-related services and other information. Offers a free clip art library of over ten thousand images. Also offers access to the Internet, which provides a gateway to discussions on nearly ten thousand different topics, including design, type and graphics software. Costs $10 per month for the first five years of use, $3 for each hour.

BITSTREAM UNDERGROUND
212 3rd Ave., N., Ste. 385
Minneapolis, MN 55401
(612) 321-9290

Features work from musicians, writers and artists in the Minneapolis area. Also offers information on local graphics and computer conferences.

COMPUSERVE
2180 Wilson Rd.
Columbus, OH 43228
(800) 848-8199, (614) 529-1340

Offers clip art, font samples and access to technical support from manufacturers of graphics software. Also provides an electronic bulletin board of questions and answers on desktop publishing matters. Costs $9 per month for unlimited use or $10 per hour.

DESIGNLINK
2034 Montclair Circle
Walnut Creek, CA 94956
(510) 930-6746

Access to industry news such as design conferences and industry magazines, virus reports, online portfolios from photographers, illustrators and designers, and more. Requires special software, available at no cost by calling (416) 299-4723. Except for the cost of a call to outside area code, the service is free for thirty minutes a day. Subscription prices are available to users wanting more access time.

DESIGN ONLINE
P.O. Box 5448
Evanston, IL 60204
(800) 326-8973, (708) 328-2733
Fax: (708) 328-1922

Offers over twenty-three fonts, available at no charge to its users, as well as portfolios. Serves as a communications hub for AIGA and AIGA services, such as its Job Bank. Cost is $45 for three months ($15 for students) plus an initial fee of $8 for the starter disk.

SOFTWARE

These are some of the best known programs available for interactive multimedia use. They combine the features of presentation software with scripting language so that text, graphics, audio and video components can be synchronized and allow for scripting sequences and creating navigational buttons. Prices are current at the time of this writing.

ADVANCED MEDIA
695 Town Center Dr., Ste. 250
Costa Mesa, CA 92626
(800) 292-4264, (714) 965-7122

Media Master (DOS, Windows)—Edits and creates audio, images and video. Creates transitions but not pull-down menus. Programming language interfaces to others. Imports AVI and MPEG videos. Price: $995.

APPLE COMPUTER
1 Infinity Loop
Cupertino, CA 95014
(800) 776-2333 (general information)

Media Director (Mac, Windows)—Enables authoring of transitions, pull-down menu creation and proprietary programming language. Can import QuickTime videos. Price: $1,495.

ATI
12638 Beatrice St.
Los Angeles, CA 90066
(800) 955-5284, (310) 823-1129

TourGuide (Windows)—Edits and creates audio, animation, images, text and video. Makes pull-down menus and transitions. Offers proprietary programming language. Can import AVI and DVI videos. Price: $2,950.

INSTANT REPLAY
Strata
2 W. St. George Blvd., Ste. 2100
St. George, UT 84770
(800) 388-8086, (801) 628-5218
Fax: (801) 628-9756

Instant Replay Professional (DOS)—Can create animation, images and audio as well as transitions and pull-down menus. Doesn't import digital video. Price: $795.

INTERSYSTEM CONCEPTS

P.O. Box 1041
Columbia, MD 21044
(410) 730-2840

Summit Authoring System (Windows)—Will create and edit images, animation and text. Can import AVI videos. Creates transitions and pull-down menus. Price: $3,695.

MACROMEDIA

P.O. Box 4100
Crawfordsville, IN 47933
(800) 989-3765, (800) 457-1774
(800) 326-2128 (literature)

Director (Mac, Windows)—Enables editing and creation of animation, images and text, pull-down menus and transitions. Can import AVI and QuickTime video. Price: $1,195.

    Authorware Professional (Mac, Windows)—Similar features to *Director*, but more sophisticated. Offers built-in training and testing features. Price: $4,995.

If you want to find out more about interactive multimedia, Multimedia Producer *is a monthly magazine published specifically for creators and developers of interactive multimedia. Contact: Montage Publishing, Inc., 701 Westchester Ave., White Plains, NY 10604; (914) 328-9157; (800) 800-5474; fax: (914) 328-9093; Internet: AVVideo@aol.com; AppleLink: kipi1.*

PASSPORT DESIGNS

100 Stone Pine Rd.
Half Moon Bay, CA 94019
(800) 443-3210, (415) 726-0280
Fax: (415) 726-2254

Passport Producer Pro (Mac)—Will create and edit animation, audio, images, text and video. Makes transitions and pull-down menus. Can import QuickTime videos. Price: $995.

PROFESSIONAL INFORMATION

Chapter

ORGANIZATIONS

AND OTHERS

WHO SERVE

GRAPHIC

DESIGN

PROFESSIONALS

GRAPHIC ARTS ORGANIZATIONS

ADVERTISING PHOTOGRAPHERS OF NEW YORK (APNY)
27 W. 20th St., #601
New York, NY 10011
(212) 807-0399

Works to increase visibility of professional photographers. Offers networking events, educational seminars and a monthly newsletter. Members receive discounts on ads in creative directories and photography supplies.

AMERICAN ASSOCIATION OF ADVERTISING AGENCIES
666 3rd Ave., 13th Fl.
New York, NY 10017
(212) 682-2500
Fax: (212) 682-8391

National association serves as a networking vehicle for the advertising industry and educates business on the value of professional advertising.

AMERICAN CENTER FOR DESIGN
233 E. Ontario St.
Chicago, IL 60611
(312) 787-2018
Fax: (312) 649-9518

A national association for design professionals, educators and students, the American Center for Design supports design education and educates the business community on the value of design.

AMERICAN FILM INSTITUTE
2021 N. Western Ave.
Los Angeles, CA 90027
(213) 856-7600
Fax: (213) 467-4578

Dedicated to the development and appreciation of motion pictures. National members receive a quarterly newsletter, access to the AFI library and discounts on AFI-sponsored seminars and special events.

THE AMERICAN INSTITUTE OF GRAPHIC ARTS (AIGA)
1059 3rd Ave.
New York, NY 10021
(212) 807-1990
Fax: (212) 807-1799

Founded in 1914, the AIGA is a nonprofit organization that promotes excellence in graphic design. The AIGA represents graphic designers on the local level with over thirty chapters in the U.S. Sponsors an annual competition and a national conference every other year.

ASSOCIATION OF MEDICAL ILLUSTRATORS
1819 Peachtree St., NE #560
Atlanta, GA 30309
(404) 350-7900
Fax: (404) 351-3348

Organization provides networking and training opportunities for medical illustrators. Sponsors full- and half-day workshops, a job hotline, and internship programs.

ASSOCIATION OF PROFESSIONAL DESIGN FIRMS (APDF)
1 Story St.
Cambridge, MA 02138
(617) 864-7474
Fax: (617) 497-6448

Comprised of firms specializing in graphic, industrial, packaging and commercial interior design, the APDF emphasizes design as a business, concentrating on networking and a candid exchange of information among member firms.

THE COLOR ASSOCIATION OF THE UNITED STATES (CAUS)
409 W. 44th St.
New York, NY 10036
(212) 582-6884
Fax: (212) 757-4557

Primarily concerned with color for fashion, interior and environmental design.

COLOR MARKETING GROUP
5904 Richmond Hwy., Ste. 408
Alexandria, VA 22303
(703) 329-8500
Fax: (703) 329-0155

A nonprofit association made up of designers, marketing experts, product developers and others whose business depends on keeping up with color trends.

GRAPHIC ARTISTS GUILD
11 W. 20th St., 8th Fl.
New York, NY 10011
(212) 463-7730
Fax: (212) 463-8779

National advocacy organization represents graphic designers, art directors, illustrators and others in the graphic design industry. Sponsors educational seminars offering advice on business aspects of the trade such as self-promotion, pricing strategies and tax issues. Promotes and maintains high professional standards of ethics and practice. Also produces the *Graphic Artists Guild Handbook: Pricing & Ethical Guidelines.*

GREETING CARD ASSOCIATION
1350 New York Ave. NW, Ste. 615
Washington, DC 20005
(202) 393-1778
Fax: (202) 393-0336

For photographers, artists and writers in the greeting card industry. Membership benefits include a monthly newsletter on industry trends and ideas.

PICTURE AGENCY COUNCIL OF AMERICA
P.O. Box 308
Northfield, MN 55057-0308
(800) 457-PACA
Fax: (507) 645-7066

Organization consists primarily of a photo stock agency. Also publishes a directory of its members, available at no charge to those who request it.

SOCIETY FOR ENVIRONMENTAL GRAPHIC DESIGN (SEGD)
1 Story St.
Cambridge, MA 02138
(617) 868-3381
Fax: (617) 868-3591

Promotes excellence in, public awareness of, and professional development in environmental graphic design. Benefits include a job bank, fabricator/designer referral service and national conference.

SOCIETY OF ILLUSTRATORS
128 E. 63rd St.
New York, NY 10010
(212) 838-2560, (212) 828-2560
Fax: (212) 838-2561

Headquarters includes a gallery that offers shows once a month of contemporary illustration. Benefits include lectures and drawing classes. Sponsors a student show and annual competition.

SOCIETY OF PHOTOGRAPHER AND ARTIST REPS (SPAR)
60 E. 42nd St., Ste. 1166
New York, NY 10065
(212) 779-7464
Fax: (203) 866-3321

Publishes a members directory and the talent they represent plus a quarterly newsletter. Also offers portfolio reviews and business forms.

The Graphic Artists Guild Handbook: Pricing & Ethical Guidelines *is widely regarded as the definitive source for contract terms, market fees, copyright information and other common trade practices for illustrators, graphic designers, and those who work with graphic arts professionals. The book includes reports on recent legislation such as the Copyright Reform Act, and offers guidelines for fee negotiation, cancellation and rejection fees, frequency rights and other ethical issues. Sample contracts and other business forms are included. You can purchase the* Handbook *at local bookstores or order it directly from the Graphic Artists Guild.*

SOCIETY OF PUBLICATION DESIGNERS
60 E. 42nd St., #721
New York, NY 10165
(212) 983-8585
Fax: (212) 983-6043

Offers monthly luncheons, speaker's evenings, and a monthly newsletter. Sponsors annual design competition and competition for best spot illustration. Also publishes an annual of award-winning work from its design competition.

TYPE DIRECTORS CLUB
60 E. 42nd St., Ste. 721
New York, NY 10065
(212) 983-6042
Fax: (212) 983-6043

Dedicated to keeping members abreast of the newest trends in typography, the club publishes a quarterly newsletter, "Letterspace." Group also sponsors a yearly competition and publishes an annual book of its award winners. Sponsors six traveling exhibitions of its competition award winners. Also holds luncheon meetings with guest speakers.

NATIONAL DIRECTORIES OF CREATIVE TALENT

These are some of the largest and best-known resource books for illustrators, photographers, designers, typographers and multimedia artists. All of them include alphabetical and regional listings as well as full-color ads that make it easy to browse for an appropriate illustration or photographic style. More details on each are available in chapter two and chapter three under the Creative Directories headings.

These directories are usually available free of charge to agencies, design studios, publishers, and others who are in a position to hire freelance talent. They can also be purchased by contacting each directly.

The Graphic Artists Guild Handbook: Pricing & Ethical Guidelines is considered by some to be an industry standard. For more information, see the top of page 127.

THE CREATIVE BLACK BOOK

10 Astor Pl., 6th Fl.
New York, NY 10003
(212) 539-9800
Fax: (212) 539-9801

Directory includes two volumes. One is devoted to listings and examples from photographers, stock photography agencies, photo labs and retouchers. The other features listings and examples from illustrators and illustrators reps.

RSVP

P.O. Box 314
Brooklyn, NY 11205
(718) 857-9267
Fax: (718) 783-2376

Publishes a directory that consists of one book divided into two sections: one each for illustration and design. Printed annually.

THE WORKBOOK

940 N. Highland Ave.
Los Angeles, CA 90038
(800) 547-2688, (213) 856-0008
Fax: (213) 856-4368
New York sales office: (212) 674-1919
Chicago sales office: (312) 944-7925

Includes listings of thousands of illustrators and photographers as well as alphabetical listings of studios, artists' reps, printers, prepress services and more. Consists of four volumes published annually.

PLACEMENT AGENCIES FOR GRAPHIC ARTS PROFESSIONALS

These agencies are in the business of matchmaking between creative professionals. Although some general employment agencies will work with graphic designers, these agencies deal exclusively with graphic designers, art directors, illustrators, production managers and professionals in related areas of design.

CHERYL ROSHAK & ASSOCIATES

141 5th Ave., 4th Fl.
New York, NY 10010
(212) 228-5050
Fax: (212) 228-5367

Bulk of placements are in the New York City area (about 75 percent). Remainder are in other major

AMERICAN SHOWCASE ILLUSTRATION

915 Broadway, 14th Fl.
New York, NY 10010
(800) 894-7469, (212) 673-6600
Fax: (212) 673-9795

Publishes two illustration volumes: one features illustrators' reps, the other features independent freelancers. Includes more than forty-five hundred images. Also publishes *Creative Options for Business and Annual Reports*, a directory that contains more than 150 images representing illustrators who do business-oriented work, and *Virtual Portfolio*, a directory of illustrators on CD-ROM. Produces a national directory of photographers and photography-related services.

U.S. cities and Japan. Firm handles a large number of computer-related positions.

CHRIS EDWARDS AGENCY, INC.
1170 Broadway
New York, NY 10001-7505
(212) 986-9400
Fax: (212) 986-6868

Handles positions in signage and exhibition, architecture and interior design as well as graphic design. Doesn't get involved in media-related positions. Bulk of placements are in New York City area, but also fills positions in other U.S. cities.

JANOU PAKTER, INC.
91 5th Ave., Rm. 201
New York, NY 10003
(212) 989-1288
Fax: (212) 989-9079

Company makes placements in New York area and other major U.S. cities, Europe, Great Britain and other parts of the world. Handles many positions that are standard to the graphic design trade and also some positions in the textile industry.

RITASUE SIEGEL RESOURCES
18 E. 48th St.
New York, NY 10017-1914
(212) 682-2100
Fax: (212) 682-2946

Handles all levels of positions in graphic, architectural, industrial, exhibit and interior design. Twenty-five percent of the agency's placements are in the New York area. Remainder are in other U.S. cities, Europe and the Far East.

ROZ GOLDFAB ASSOCIATES
10 E. 22nd St., 4th Fl.
New York, NY 10010
(212) 475-0099
Fax: (212) 473-8096

Agency makes placements in architecture, interior design, industrial design and graphic design. Bulk of business is in New York City.

STONE & CO.
Forbes Business Center
222 Forbes Rd., Ste. 406
Braintree, MA 02184
(617) 356-7001
Fax: (617) 356-7007

Founded in 1959, this agency is the oldest placement agency in the country specializing exclusively in design. Handles placements in major U.S. cities as well as some overseas businesses.

COMPETITIONS

Deadline dates listed are current at the time of publication, but can vary from one year to the next. Call sponsoring organizations for up-to-date deadlines, contact and other information, and entry forms.

ADDY'S
American Advertising Federation
(800) 999-2231
Deadline: mid-April

ADLA ANNUAL EXHIBITION
Art Directors Club of Los Angeles
(213) 465-8707
Call for deadline

AIGA COMMUNICATION GRAPHICS EXHIBIT
American Institute of Graphic Arts
(212) 752-0813
Call for deadline

ART DIRECTORS CLUB ANNUAL EXHIBITION
(212) 674-0500
Deadline: early December

AWARDS SHOW FOR PRINT AND RADIO
New York Festivals
(914) 238-4481
Deadline: mid-June

BEACON AWARDS
American Center for Design/*Fortune* magazine
(800) 257-8657, (312) 787-2018
Deadline: mid-November

BLACK BOOK AWARDS
Black Book Marketing
(212) 702-9700
Deadline: mid-April

COMMUNICATION ARTS (CA) DESIGN ANNUAL
Communication Arts magazine
(415) 326-6040
Deadline: mid-June

"FRESH IDEAS" SERIES OF GRAPHIC DESIGN BOOKS
North Light Books
(800) 289-0963, (513) 531-2690 x277
Deadline: biennial

HOW INTERNATIONAL ANNUAL OF DESIGN
HOW magazine
(800) 289-0963, (513) 531-2690
Deadline: late September

HOW SELF-PROMOTION CONTEST
HOW magazine
(800) 289-0963, (513) 531-2690
Deadline: mid-March

INTERNATIONAL INTERACTIVE MULTIMEDIA AWARDS
New York Festivals
(914) 238-4481
Deadline: mid-May

INTERNATIONAL TV AND CINEMA ADVERTISING AWARDS
New York Festivals
(914) 238-4481
Deadlines: late June, mid-September

KUDOS FROM HOPPER INTERNATIONAL DESIGN COMPETITION
Hopper Paper/Georgia Pacific Corp.
(212) 868-2727
Deadline: late October

LETTERHEAD OF THE YEAR COMPETITION
Gilbert Paper Co.
(414) 729-7630
Deadline: late December

LITERARY MARKETPLACE AWARDS
Reed Reference Publishing
(800) 5-BOWKER
Deadline: mid-November

MEAD ANNUAL REPORT SHOW
(800) 345-6323
Deadline: late May

MOBIUS ADVERTISING AWARDS
U.S. Festivals Association
(708) 834-7773
Deadline: early October

NEA INDIVIDUAL GRANTS FOR DESIGN INNOVATION AND USA FELLOWSHIPS
National Endowment for the Arts
(202) 682-5437
Deadline: mid-June

THE ONE SHOW
The One Club
(212) 255-7070
Deadline: late January

THE 100 SHOW
American Center for Design
(800) 257-8657, (312) 787-2018
Deadline: May

PRESIDENTIAL DESIGN AWARD
National Endowment for the Arts
(202) 682-5437
Deadline: late October

PIA GRAPHIC ARTS AWARDS
Printing Industries of America
(703) 519-8100
Deadline: late April

PRINT'S REGIONAL DESIGN ANNUAL
Print magazine
(212) 463-0600
Deadline: mid-March

SEGD ANNUAL COMPETITION
Society of Environmental Graphic Designers
(617) 868-3381
Deadline: mid-April

SOCIETY OF ILLUSTRATORS ANNUAL COMPETITION
Society of Illustrators
(800) 746-8738, (212) 838-2560
Deadline: early October

SOCIETY OF PUBLICATION DESIGNERS ANNUAL COMPETITION
Society of Publication Designers, Inc.
(212) 983-8585
Deadline: mid-January

STRATHMORE GRAPHICS GALLERY
Strathmore Paper Co.
(203) 677-8821
Deadline: ongoing

TDC ANNUAL AWARDS
Type Directors Club
(212) 983-6042
Deadline: mid-January

TOUCHSTONE AWARDS
American Society for Health Marketing &
PR of the American Hospital Association
(312) 280-6359
Deadline: early May

UCDA AWARDS
University & College Designers Association
(219) 586-2988
Deadline: June

U.S. INTERNATIONAL FILM & VIDEO FESTIVAL
U.S. Festivals
(708) 834-7773
Deadline: early March

MAGAZINES/ NEWSLETTERS

The publications listed below are all available on a subscription basis—in addition, some can be purchased at newsstands or art supply stores. Subscription prices listed below do not reflect promotional specials that are often found within a given magazine.

ADVERTISING AGE
220 E. 42nd St.
New York, NY 10017
(800) 992-9970, (212) 210-0205
Fax: (313) 446-6777

National weekly advertising and marketing news publication. Yearly subscription is $99.

APPLIED ARTS QUARTERLY
885 Don Millis Rd., #324
Don Millis, Ontario M3C 1V9
Canada
(416) 510-0909
Fax: (416) 510-0909

Published in January, April, July and October, magazine features freelance talent in illustration, photography, lettering, type design and art direction. Also includes reps and retouching. Yearly subscription is $64.

THE ART OF SELF-PROMOTION
P.O. Box 23
Hoboken, NJ 07030-0023
(800) 737-0783, (201) 653-0783
Fax: (201) 222-2494

Quarterly newsletter published by self-promotion specialist Ilise Benun. Includes tips on topics such as writing press releases, creating a mailing list and cold calling. Cost is $25 for four issues.

AV VIDEO
701 Westchester Ave.
White Plains, NY 10604
(914) 328-9157
Fax: (914) 328-9093

Features multimedia, video, audio and computer graphics information. Published monthly, the magazine has a controlled circulation and is only available to those who qualify for a subscription.

BOARD REPORT
P.O. Box 300789
Denver, CO 80203
(303) 839-9058

Monthly newsletter features techniques and practical advice on producing better and more cost-effective graphic design projects. Subscription includes *Graphic Artists Newsletter*, *Designer's Compendium* and *Trademark Trends*, a monthly review of exciting new logo designs. Yearly subscription is $96 with a six-month guarantee.

COMMUNICATION ARTS
410 Sherman Ave.
P.O. Box 10300
Palo Alto, CA 94306-1826
(415) 326-6040
Fax: (415) 326-1648

One of the design industry's most venerable journals, showcases top U.S. design and illustration talent. Publishes three annuals per year. Published eight times a year. Yearly subscription: $50.

CREATIVE BUSINESS
233 W. Canton St.
Boston, MA 02116
(617) 424-1368
Fax: (617) 353-1391

Published by freelance expert Cameron Foote, this newsletter is about the business side of freelancing. Published ten times a year, it offers tips on making a small creative business successful. Annual subscription is $79.

DESIGN WORLD
% Eastern News Distributors, Inc.
1130 Cleveland Rd.
Sandusky, OH 44870
(419) 627-0134
Fax: (419) 627-1311

Monthly journal on international design published out of Austrialia. Can be purchased in the U.S. for $7.95 per issue.

EMIGRE
4475 D St.
Sacramento, CA 95819
(800) 944-9021, (916) 451-4344
Fax: (916) 451-4351

Quarterly tabloid showcases work of type designers, illustrators and others whose work is on the cutting edge of the creative community. Unique design and typographic approaches are noteworthy. *Emigre* also markets the typefaces in its magazine and picture fonts. (See listings in chapters two and four.) Yearly subscription is $28.

GRAPHIC DESIGN: USA
1556 3rd Ave., Ste. 405
New York, NY 10128
(212) 534-5500
Fax: (212) 534-4415

Monthly magazine features news and ideas for graphic designers and art directors. Yearly subscription is $60; $5 per issue.

GRAPHIS
141 Lexington Ave.
New York, NY 10016
(212) 532-9387
Fax: (212) 213-3229

Bimonthly design magazine acclaimed for its artistic presentation of showcased work. Includes news, profiles, commentary and features. Yearly subscription: $89; $18.75 per issue.

HOW
1507 Dana Ave.
Cincinnati, OH 45207
(800) 365-0963, (513) 531-2690
Fax: (513) 531-4744

Bimonthly graphic design magazine covering ideas, techniques, and other aspects of the trade. Well-known for its popular business annual, which focuses on successful design studios and freelancers across the U.S. Sponsors competitions and an annual conference. Yearly subscription: $49; $7 per issue; $12 for business annual.

I.D. MAGAZINE
440 Park Ave., S., Fl. 14
New York, NY 10016
(212) 447-1400
Fax: (212) 447-5231

Explores current issues and trends in graphic, product and environmental design. Sponsors an-

nual competition for design excellence. Published seven times a year. Yearly subscription is $60.

IDENTITY
407 Gilbert Ave.
Cincinnati, OH 45202
(513) 421-2050
Fax: (513) 421-5144

For environmental graphic designers. Includes case studies of projects by well-known design firms. Published bimonthly. Yearly subscription: $24; $5 per issue.

LUZER'S INTERNATIONAL ARCHIVE
915 Broadway, 14th Fl.
New York, NY 10010
(800) 894-7469, (212) 673-6600
Fax: (212) 673-9795

Features the best advertising from around the world. Published bimonthly. Yearly subscription is $48.

MACUSER
Ziff Davis
P.O. Box 56986
Boulder, CO 80322
(303) 604-1464
Fax: (303) 604-7455

Monthly magazine dedicated to reporting trends and tips on getting optimum performance from Macintosh computers, Mac-compatible software and other related products. Annual subscription is $27; single issue is $2.25.

MACWORLD
P.O. Box 54529
Boulder, CO 80322-4529
(800) 288-6848, (303) 604-1465

Reports on trends, new technology and tips that improve Macintosh computing. Features focus on best upgrade alternatives, latest software and other newsworthy items. Published monthly, yearly subscription is $24; single issue price is $4.95.

PRE MAGAZINE
℅ Cowles Business Media
470 Park Ave. S., 7th Fl., North Tower
New York, NY 10016
(212) 683-3540
Fax: (212) 683-4572

This monthly covers aspects of communication design and production that are specific to magazines and other publications. Sponsors the Ozzies, an annual competition for the best in magazine design. A yearly subscription is $45.

PRINT

3200 Tower Oaks Blvd.
Rockville, MD 20852-9789
(800) 222-2654, (301) 770-2900
Fax: (301) 984-3203

Covering the graphic design industry for over 50 years, *Print* covers all aspects of the business and publishes a yearly annual of top design work. Sponsors annual competition and national seminars. Published bimonthly. Yearly subscription: $55; $34 for design annual.

PUBLISH

501 2nd St.
San Francisco, CA 94107
(800) 656-7495, (415) 243-0600
Fax: (415) 495-2354

Bimonthly dedicated to graphic design in electronic communication. Includes technological updates and production tips for computer publishing, interactives and other aspects of digital design. Yearly subscription is $23.95; single issue price is $6.

STEP-BY-STEP ELECTRONIC DESIGN

6000 N. Forest Park Dr.
Peoria, IL 61614-3592
(309) 698-0001
Fax: (309) 698-0831

Monthly periodical takes reader through step-by-step digital production of design projects. Yearly subscription: $48.

STEP-BY-STEP GRAPHICS

6000 N. Forest Park Dr.
Peoria, IL 61614-3592
(309) 698-0001
Fax: (309) 698-0831

Bimonthly magazine focuses on how well-known designers, photographers, illustrators and other graphic arts professionals create a project. Yearly subscription: $42; $7.50 per issue.

STUDIO MAGAZINE

124 Galaxy Blvd.
Rexdale, Ontario M9W 4Y6
Canada
(416) 675-1999
Fax: (416) 675-6093

Canada's international magazine for visual communications. Includes in-depth profiles, features and news for the industry. Published seven times a year; the December annual showcases the winning work of their yearly competition. Yearly subscription: $40; $7.95 per issue; $17 for awards annual.

U&lc

866 2nd Ave.
New York, NY 10017
(212) 371-0699
Fax: (212) 752-4752

Published quarterly by International Typeface Corp., this tabloid includes news, features and profiles. Focus is on trends in typographic design and production. Subscription price is $14 per year.

WINDOWS MAGAZINE

600 Community Dr.
Manhasset, NY 11030
(800) 829-9150, (516) 562-5000
Fax: (904) 445-2728

Dedicated to reporting on trends and tips that help professionals working with Windows computing. Includes information on latest software and hardware developments. Published monthly, annual subscription is $24.94; single issue is $2.95.

WIRED

544 2nd St.
San Francisco, CA 94107-1427
(415) 904-0660
Fax: (415) 904-0669

Monthly magazine promotes and reports on technological innovations in digital communication. Features focus on newsworthy topics that affect computer publishing, multimedia and communicating on the Internet. Social commentary and trendy graphics reflect current pop culture. Yearly subscription is $39.95; single issue price is $4.95.

PUBLISHERS OF DESIGN BOOKS

If you need some resources for expertise, inspiration or other help in your work, call these publishers. All of them specialize in books for graphic artists and will send a free catalog.

ADOBE PRESS

1585 Charleston Rd.
P.O. Box 7900
Mountain View, CA 94039-7900
(800) 344-8335, (415) 961-4400

This software and font manufacturer now offers books, many of them co-authored by the authors of the software. Offerings include books on imaging techniques that give step-by-step instructions on how to use Adobe Illustrator and Adobe Photoshop. Covers information that user's manuals fail to cover.

ART DIRECTION BOOK CO.

10 E. 39th St.
New York, NY 10016
(212) 889-6500
Fax: (212) 889-6504

Specializes in books for graphic designers, illustrators, art directors and production artists. Offerings include *Graphics Master*, books of symbols and how-to books.

CHRONICLE BOOKS

275 5th St.
San Francisco, CA 94103
(800) 722-6657, (415) 777-8467
Fax: (800) 858-7787

Offers books on design, including many nostalgic subjects, such as vintage trademarks, signs and letterheads, and titles with a unique sense of funk. Some books showcase offbeat subject matter, such as tobacco accoutrements and board games of the fifties.

DESIGN PRESS

10 E. 21st St.
New York, NY 10010
(212) 512-2000, (800) 722-4726, (800) 338-3987

A subsidiary of McGraw-Hill, this division offers titles that cover academic and historical perspectives on design.

DOVER PUBLICATIONS, INC.

31 E. 2nd St.
Mineola, NY 11501
(516) 294-7000

In addition to clip art books, Dover's Pictorial Archive catalog offers over six hundred books that feature vintage graphics, illustration and photography, organized by category. Offerings include items such as reproductions of period patterns and borders. Company also offers note cards, gift wrap and other items with a vintage theme.

MADISON SQUARE PRESS

10 E. 23rd St.
New York, NY 10010
(212) 505-0950
Fax: (212) 979-2207

Specializes in showcasing outstanding work in different areas of design. Offers hard-bound, four-

color books on typography, environmental graphics and more.

NORTH LIGHT BOOKS

1507 Dana Ave.
Cincinnati, OH 45207
(800) 289-0963, (513) 531-2690
Fax: (513) 531-4744

Specializes in books for graphic designers that are both instructional and inspiring. Offers step-by-step technique, idea and creativity books, reference books, business books and more. Also distributes other imprints (including computer instruction and reference, showcases of great design work and specialty topics) through the Graphic Design Book Club.

PEACHPIT PRESS

2414 6th St.
Berkeley, CA 94710
(800) 283-9444, (510) 548-4393
Fax: (510) 548-5991

Publishes books on computer graphics, the Internet, virtual reality and practical issues for computer designers. Offers some excellent guides to graphics software that go beyond the information found in conventional user's manuals.

PRINT BOOKS

RC Publications, Inc.
3200 Tower Oaks Blvd.
Rockville, MD 20852
(800) 222-2654
Fax: (301) 984-3203

Offers many types of books for graphic designers and illustrators. Specializes in "Print's Best" and case story books that feature winners from *Print* magazine's annual regional competition.

RIZZOLI INTERNATIONAL

300 Park Ave., S., 5th Fl.
New York, NY 10010
(212) 387-3400

Specializes in showcase books that feature outstanding design from Europe, Great Britain and other overseas markets. Has two retail locations in New York City.

ROCKPORT PUBLISHERS, INC.

146 Granite St.
Rockport, MA 01966
(508) 546-9590
Fax: (508) 546-7141

Publishes many types of design books but specializes in showcase books that feature outstanding work in a particular area of graphic design such as businesss cards, shopping bags, direct mail design, etc.

ST PUBLICATIONS

407 Gilbert Ave.
Cincinnati, OH 45202
(800) 925-1110, (513) 421-2050
Fax: (513) 421-5144

Specializes in books on environmental graphics, signage, display and screen printing. Offerings include the AIGA's book on symbol signs for the Department of Transportation and a camera-ready portfolio of D.O.T. symbols.

VANNOSTRAND REINHOLD

115 E. 5th Ave.
New York, NY 10003
(212) 254-3232
(606) 525-6600 (for catalog and orders)
Fax: (606) 525-7778

Publishes many books on graphic design and illustration. Titles focus on contemporary issues and designers as well as historical subject matter. Offers instructional as well as showcase books.

WATSON-GUPTILL

515 Broadway
New York, NY 10036
(212) 764-7300
(212) 536-5127 (for editorial questions)
(908) 363-4511 (for catalog and orders)

Offers a wide variety of instructional books for graphic designers.

ONLINE SERVICES

If your computer has a modem, the following services will give you access to design-related products and services.

AMERICA ONLINE

8619 Westwood Center Dr.
Vienna, VA 22182-2285
(800) 827-6364, (703) 448-8700

Access through e-mail to other design firms, design-related services and other information. Also offers a free clip art library of over ten thousand images and access to the Internet, which provides a gateway to discussions on nearly ten thousand different topics, including design, type and graphics software. Costs $10 per month for five years of use, $3 per hour.

COMPUSERVE

2180 Wilson Rd.
Columbus, OH 43228
(800) 848-8199, (614) 457-8600

Offers clip art, font samples, and access to technical support from manufacturers of graphics software. Also provides an electronic bulletin board of questions and answers on desktop publishing matters. Costs $9 per month for unlimited use or $10 per hour.

DESIGNLINK

2034 Montclair Cr.
Walnut Creek, CA 94596
(510) 930-6746

Access to industry news such as design conferences and industry magazines, virus reports, online portfolios from photographers, illustrators and designers, and more. Requires special software, available at no cost by calling (416) 299-4723. Except for cost of call to outside area code, the service is free for thirty minutes a day. Subscription prices are available to users wanting more access time.

DESIGN ONLINE

804 Dempster St.
Evanston, IL 60202
(800) 326-8973

Offers over twenty-three fonts, available at no charge to its users, as well as portfolios. Serves as a communications hub for AIGA and AIGA services, such as its Job Bank. Cost is $45 for three months ($15 for students) plus an initial fee of $8 for the starter disk.

TIP

Want to find out more about online services for creative professionals and how to put them to work for you? Check out *U&lc*'s article, ''Online Design,'' by David Pogue, Winter, 1994.

Dear Graphic Designer:

Wouldn't you like to see even *more* helpful information—all in the same place, right at your fingertips when you need it? We want to make the next edition of *The Graphic Designer's Sourcebook* even better than this one, and with a little help from you, we can be sure to print more of the information that you and your colleagues really need. Please use the following form to let us know about new suppliers, old favorites we might have missed, corrections or updates you know about, or even fresh news about a company already listed. Photocopy as many copies as you want—we want your input so we can make this *the* sourcebook you turn to—time and time again.

Dear *Graphic Designer's Sourcebook* Editor:

I'd really like to help you improve your next edition of *The Graphic Designer's Sourcebook*. The following additions are resources I'd like to share with my colleagues:

1. Name of company _____

   Address _____

   _____

   Phone number(s) (800) _____ (toll-free)   (   )_____ (local)

   Fax number(s) (800) _____ (toll-free)   (   )_____ (local)

   Product(s) and/or service(s) _____

   _____

   _____

   _____

   Other important information _____

   _____

   _____

2. Name of company _____

   Address _____

   _____

   Phone number(s) (800) _____ (toll-free)   (   )_____ (local)

   Fax number(s) (800) _____ (toll-free)   (   )_____ (local)

   Product(s) and/or service(s) _____

   _____

   _____

   _____

   Other important information _____

   _____

   _____

INDEX

More Great Books for Graphic Designers!

1996 Artist's & Graphic Designer's Market—This marketing tool for fine artists and graphic designers includes listings of 2,500 buyers across the country and helpful advice on selling and showing your work from top art and design professionals. *#10434/$23.99/720 pages*

Graphic Design: Inspirations and Innovations—Seventy-five of America's top designers discuss how they work, the creative process and the client relationship. Included are discussions on where ideas come from, how to work out your ideas and selling ideas to the client. *#30710/$28.99/144 pages/201 color, 49 b&w illus.*

Graphic Design Basics: Marketing and Promoting Your Work—This practical guide covers the marketing essentials you need to get the word out on your work. Throughout, successful designers share their own "Super Strategies" for marketing—proven ideas on such topics as establishing recognition and avoiding miscommunication with clients. *#30706/$27.99/128 pages/25 color, 10 b&w illus.*

Make Your Scanner a Great Design & Production Tool—Discover powerful techniques and time-saving tips to help you get quick, clean scans and "just right" images. You'll learn how to make the most of your scanning equipment with step-by-step instructions on everything from cleaning up undesirable moiré patterns to creating special effects. *#30661/$27.99/144 pages/117 color, 103 b&w illus./paperback*

Graphic Design Basics: Creating Logos & Letterheads—Using 14 creativity-sparking, step-by-step demonstrations, Jennifer Place shows you how to make logos, letterheads and business cards that speak out about a client and pack a visual punch. *#30616/$27.99/128 pages/110 color, 125 b&w illus.*

Creating Great Designs on a Limited Budget—This studio manual, written by two authors who know design and its penny-pinching realities, shows designers how to create topflight work, even when the dollars are few. You'll discover how to create impact using only one or two colors, ways to get high mileage from low-cost visuals, thrifty ways to get jobs produced and many other money-saving tips. *#30711/$28.99/128 pages/ 133 color, 27 b&w illus.*

The Designer's Commonsense Business Book, Revised Edition—Find guidance on setting up shop, networking, pricing, self-promotion and record keeping to help you meet your long-term goals. Completely updated and revised, this book will help you learn the nuts-and-bolts business practices for freelance success. *#30663/$27.99/224 pages/paperback*

Graphic Idea Notebook—This innovative, problem-solving source book for magazine editors and art directors provides over 1,000 editorial design ideas. *#30303/$19.95/206 pages/1,250 b&w illus./paperback*

More Great Design Using 1, 2 & 3 Colors—Discover the graphic impact possible using fewer colors—and spending fewer dollars! In this follow-up edition, you will see how limiting your color choices to one, two or three colors can help you make strong, creative graphics choices that keep your standards high and your expenses low. *#30664/$39.95/192 pages/225 color illus.*

Graphic Edge—This bold international collection explores nontraditional ways of using type. Over 250 color images of typographic rebellions from top designers are presented. *#30733/$34.95/208 pages/280 color illus./paperback*

Getting Started in Computer Graphics—A hands-on guide for designers and illustrators with more than 200 state-of-the-art examples. Software includes Adobe Photoshop, Fractal Design Painter, Aldus FreeHand, Adobe Illustrator, PixelPaint and Micrografx Designer. *#30469/$27.95/160 pages/125 color, 25 b&w illus./paperback*

Getting It Printed—Discover practical, hands-on advice for working with printers and graphic arts services to ensure the down and dirty details like consistent quality, on-time output and effective cost control. *#30552/$29.99/208 pages/134 color, 48 b&w illus./paperback*

Fresh Ideas in Promotion—Whenever you need a shot of creativity this knockout collection of everything from brochures and newsletters to packaging and wearables will bring you the freshest ideas for a variety of clients (and budgets)! *#30634/$29.99/144 pages/220 color illus.*

Setting the Right Price for Your Design and Illustration—Don't price yourself out of work or vital income. Easy-to-use worksheets show you how to set the right hourly rate plus how to price a variety of assignments! *#30615/$24.99/160 pages/ paperback*

Getting Unlimited Impact with Limited Color—Discover how to deliver high-impact colors on a budget by mixing two screen tints, replacing four-color photos with duotones or tritones and dozens of other techniques! *#30612/$27.99/ 144 pages/120 color illus.*

Graphic Artist's Guild Handbook of Pricing & Ethical Guidelines, 8th Edition—You'll get practical advice on how to negotiate fees, the ins and outs of trade practices, the latest tax advice and more. *#30574/$24.95/240 pages/paperback*

Quick Solutions for Great Type Combinations—When you're looking for that "just right" type combination and you don't have the time or money to experiment endlessly, here's hundreds of ideas to create the mood you're after, including all specs. *#30571/$26.99/144 pages/175 b&w illus./paperback*

Collage with Photoshop—Step-by-step demonstrations will show you how to create cutting-edge images using Specular International's image composition software, Collage, with Adobe Photoshop, Fractal Painter and other digital imaging programs. This astonishing collection of projects provides you in-depth instruction and inspiration to absorb into your own digital imaging skills. *#30735/$39.99/205 pages/700 color illus./paperback*

Fresh Ideas in Letterhead & Business Card Design 2—A great idea-sparker for your own letterhead, envelope and business card designs. One hundred twenty sets shown large, in color and with notes on concepts, production and costs. *#30660/$29.99/144 pages/325 color illus.*

Using Type Right—One hundred twenty-one no-nonsense guidelines for designing with type. Dozens of examples demonstrate good versus bad type design and help you make the statement you want. *#30071/$18.95/120 pages/paperback*

Basic Desktop Design and Layout—This book shows you how to maximize your desktop publishing potential and use any desktop system to produce designs quickly. *#30130/$27.95/160 pages/ 50 color, 100 b&w illus./paperback*

Graphic Design Basics: Making a Good Layout—Discover how to create more effective layouts that attract the viewer's attention, organize information and fulfill the purpose of the piece. In five highly illustrated chapters, you'll learn how to identify a good layout and how to use the elements and principles of design effectively. Then you'll practice what you learn by working side by side with the authors as they create a sample layout for an actual project. *#30364/$24.99/128 pages/40 color, 100 b&w illus.*

Color on Color—Shows what colors can be created simply by overprinting one color over another. Includes 100 pages of colors, each reproduced in solid coverage, 50% screen and 20% screen, plus 11 acetates. *#30467/$34.95/160 pages + 11 acetates*

Great Type & Lettering Designs—A lively showcase of innovative and successful typographic designs applied to all printed media, including publications, packaging, logos, promotion and posters. *#30419/$34.99/160 pages/175 illus.*

Color Harmony 2: A Guide to Creative Color Combinations—Discover 1,400 fresh color combinations that make choosing mood-evoking colors a cinch in 2 and 3 color work! Plus, an easy conversion chart is your key to process color percentages. *#30584/15.95/160 pages/ 500+ color swatches/paperback*

Graphic Design Basics: Working with Words & Pictures—Learn how to make type an attractive, effective communication tool and how to use visuals and graphics to beautify and communicate. In 150 examples, you'll discover achievable designs offering instructions and tips you can put to work in your own designs. *#30515/$26.99/128 pages/32 color, 195 b&w illus.*

Fresh Ideas in Letterhead and Business Card Design—A great idea-sparker for your own letterhead, envelope and business card designs. One hundred twenty sets shown large and in color with notes on concepts, production and costs. *#30481/$29.99/144 pages/125 color illus.*

Newsletter Sourcebook—Everything you need to produce an effective newsletter, including creative design tips, easy editorial cost savers, proven production and distribution techniques and solid advice for smart money management. *#30488/$26.99/144 pages/45 color, 160 b&w illus.*

Fresh Ideas in Corporate Identity: Logos & Their Applications— Get an insider's look at more than 80 knockout corporate identity systems from firms like Pentagram, Vaughn Wedeen, Clement Mok Designs and others. You'll see over 200 examples of logos, letterheads, posters and more—all in full-color and in an array of applications. *#30569/$29.99/ 144 pages/160 color illus.*

Quick Solutions to Great Layouts—Get your creative juices flowing with hundreds of time-saving ideas! You'll find sample cases with real-world solutions including full specs for newsletters, brochures, ads and more! *#30529/$24.99/ 144 pages/200 illus.*

Graphic Design Basics: Creating Brochures and Booklets—Detailed demonstrations show you precisely how to plan, design and produce everything from a church bulletin to a four-color brochure. Plus, a full-color gallery of 20 well-designed brochures and booklets will give you loads of inspiration. *#30568/$26.99/ 128 pages/60 color, 145 b&w illus.*

The Graphic Artist's Guide to Marketing and Self-Promotion—Get the most from your efforts and talent! Firsthand experiences of other designers and illustrators show you exactly what to do and what to avoid. *#30353/$19.99/128 pages/ 81 b&w illus./paperback*

Creativity for Graphic Designers—If you're burned-out or just plain stuck for ideas, this book will help you spark your creativity and find the best idea for any project. *#30659/$29.99/144 pages/169 color illus.*

How to Get Great Type Out of Your Computer—One hundred twelve time-and-money saving tips for designers and desktop publishers. *#30360/$22.95/138 pages/50 b&w illus./paperback*

Complete Process Color Finder—Take the guesswork out of color printing jobs. Complete process color samples with graduated tints and shades for each color, enable this guide to provide you with a full range of creative color choices. *#30677/$24.99/182 pages/full-color throughout*